Basic Bible Sermons on Christian Stewardship

BASIC BIBLE SERMONS

ON

CHRISTIAN STEWARDSHIP

J. Alfred Smith, Sr.
with J. Alfred Smith, Jr.

BROADMAN PRESS
NASHVILLE, TENNESSEE

Dewey Decimal Classification: 248.6
Subject Heading: STEWARDSHIP—SERMONS
Library of Congress Catalog Card Number: 92-12655
Printed in the United States of America

All Scripture references, unless otherwise indicated, are from the *King James Version* of the Holy Bible. All Scripture references marked GNB are from the *Good News Bible*, the Bible in Today's English Version. Old Testament: Copyright © American Bible Society 1976; New Testament: Copyright © American Bible Society 1966, 1971, 1976. Used by permission.

Library of Congress Cataloging-in-Publication Data

Smith, J. Alfred (James Alfred)
   Basic Bible sermons on Christian stewardship / J. Alfred Smith, Sr.
with J. Alfred Smith, Jr.
     p.   cm.
   ISBN 0-8054-2006-1
   1. Stewardship, Christian—Sermons. 2. Christian giving—Sermons.
3. Sermons, American. 4. Baptists—Sermons. I. Smith, J. Alfred
(James Alfred), 1952–   II. Title.
BV772.S613   1992
248'.6—dc20   92-12655
                                                    CIP

Dedicated
to JoAnna and Elaine
our
wives
who
are
constructive
critics
and loving supporters
of
our
preaching

Acknowledgments

The messages in this manuscript are based on a high view of Scripture. They express the cardinal principles of stewardship that flow from the Bible. These sermons do not express the moralisms of secular philosophy and literature since the Bible is the absolute rule and guide for our faith and practice.

I am deeply grateful to the staff of Broadman Press for prayerfully and patiently encouraging and guiding us in the preparation of the manuscript. I am also grateful to Copastor J. Alfred Smith, Jr., of Allen Temple Baptist Church of Oakland, California, for contributing some of his stewardship sermons to the manuscript. Mrs. Mildred Rose is to be commended for typing each word of the text from the hard-to-read handwriting submitted to her by both J. Alfred Smith, Jr., and me.

A sabbatical spent at Fuller Theological Seminary in Pasadena, California, allowed me to work on the completion of the manuscript. Doctor William Dryness, dean of the School of Theology of Fuller, provided me with living quarters and office space so I could write with the emotional and spiritual support of my wife, JoAnna Goodwin Smith. I am grateful to God for the opportunity to serve as a steward of the sacred Word.

—*J. Alfred Smith, Sr.*

Preface

The sermons in this manuscript were warmly received by the members of the Allen Temple Baptist Church of Oakland, California. They became topics of discussion in Church School classes, Home Bible study groups, and the Pastor's Bible class. A few of the members were gracious enough to send letters of encouragement and appreciation. We are convinced that the pew can either encourage or discourage persons who preach from the pulpit. We are grateful to God for positive listeners who pray for those who preach in the Allen Temple pulpit.

Although written sermons do not carry the intensity and power of the spoken word, it is our prayer that God will use these sermons to touch hearts, and to persuade readers to accept the Christian message and to allow Jesus Christ to become The Lord of their lives. We offer these messages to you in humility and love.

Pastor J. Alfred Smith, Sr.
Copastor J. Alfred Smith, Jr.

Contents

1
Hope for the Country of the Blind

In him was life, and the life was the light of men. The light shines in the darkness, and the darkness has not overcome it (John 1:4-5, RSV).

And out of their gloom and darkness the eyes of the blind shall see (Isa. 29:18b, RSV).

The famous Margaret Mead said: "The land of our life is in disorder." Because her words are true, we now live in the country of the blind. Recently at a leadership conference for pastors in Chicago, Dr. Thomas Kilgore spoke of the inexorable cycle which moves us from spiritual values to non-spiritual values. Dr. Kilgore said, "Such behavior will lead us away from deliverance to destruction."

In our country of the blind, the moral eye has no need for the Ten Commandments. The light of truth which shines from the Sermon on the Mount, the rays of sunlight which radiate from sacred Scriptures, and the brightness of the teachings of Jesus Christ have not been allowed to help our nation lead the rest of the world from the dungeon of darkness.

America may lead the world with her powerful dollar and rich economy. She may stand at the top of the ladder of scientific and intellectual success. Her military power may be second to none, but as a nonviolent, God-loving, moral leader, America must move to the head of the class of embarrassment. For instead of being one nation under God's holy light, she is a country of the blind dwelling not far from the destruction of a spiritual midnight.

Our spiritual blindness and moral darkness are of unparalleled proportions. Each day television and radio inform us of fresh evils, and new temptations to greed and power. In our country of the blind, stones of immorality and rocks of disrespect fill the pathway causing the sightless good to stumble and fall.

In our country of the blind, citizens can no longer behold the beauty of dignity or the attractiveness of honesty. Disorder, destruction, death, and demoralizing and degrading values have far more at-homeness and acceptability than goodness, truth, and beauty. An unknown philosopher said, "in the country of the blind, the one-eyed man is King." In our world, however, not too many one-eyed men are left.

Our one-eyed men are dangerous pilots, trying to land the 747s of the nation on moral runways that are foggy with confusion. Our one-eyed men are surgeons, trying to cut the cancerous tissue of immorality out of the body of the country, while the poorly lit candle of Christianity provides dim hope in a dark operating room. Times like these remind us of the words Jesus, our Lord, spoke in Matthew 15:14: "Let them alone; they are blind guides. And if a blind man leads a blind man, both will fall into a pit" (RSV).

Sometimes people are not completely blind when they fall into the ditch. The optic nerve of their soul has not been destroyed. Their problem is that they are nearsighted. They can see themselves, but they cannot see others. God made me not for myself alone. He made me not to get for myself alone. People need each other. Hear God's Word, "Bear ye one another's burdens, and so fulfill the law of Christ" (Gal. 6:2).

You may not be nearsighted. You may see your brothers and sisters, but you are so farsighted that your own sins and shortcomings are obvious to everyone except you. Can we see as those first disciples who each examined himself, asking, "Lord, is it I?" (Matt. 26:22).

Our denomination believes that the Lord's Supper is the time when each person prays "Lord, is it I?" During holy communion, fathers don't pray for daughters, and mothers don't pray for sons, but each one prays, "It's me, it's me, it's me, O Lord, Standin' in the need of prayer."

In the country of the blind, the inability of self-examination marries the lady of forgetfulness. From this union comes the child of ingratitude. When you forget to see that you don't deserve God's blessings, your forgetfulness and your marred, scarred, self-pity produce the blindness of thanklessness.

It is the blind person who can't say, "I thank you Jesus, I thank you Lord! You have been better to me than I have been to myself." It is the blind person who becomes so self-centered as to ignore God. Only the blind disregards the love of God and disavows the mercy of God.

Have you ever awakened in the middle of the night, turned on the light, and immediately turned the light back off because the brightness hurt your eyes? When you have spent time in darkness, strong light hurts your eyes. The strong light of truth hurts the eyes of the soul that live in darkness rather than light. When you leave the cave of falsehood, when you divest yourself of the dungeon of degradation, the eyes of the soul are pained by the daylight of the gospel.

Only by walking in the daylight of Christian fellowship will this world have hope. Fellowship is *fellows in the ship together.* According to 1 John 1:5-10, true fellowship is the result of walking in the light of Christ. Hear John:

> This is the message we have heard from him, and proclaim to you, that God is light and in him is no darkness at all. If we say we have fellowship with him while we walk in darkness, we lie and do not live according to the truth; but if we walk in the light, as he is in the light, we have fellowship with one another, and the blood of Jesus his Son cleanses us from all sin. If we say we have no sin, we deceive ourselves, and the truth is not in us. If we confess our sins, he is faithful and just, and will forgive our sins, and cleanse us from all unrighteousness. If we say we have not sinned, we make him a liar, and his word is not in us (RSV).

The apostle John gives us hope. He lets us know that in our country of the blind, Jesus Christ is our hope. To follow Jesus is to accept One who can open eyes blinded by sin. Jesus is the Light Giver who said, "As long as I am in the world, I am the light of the world" (John 9:5). Jesus is not the leading light for the country of the blind—Jesus is the *only* Light!

> We'll walk in the light, beautiful light, come where the dewdrops of mercy are bright, Shine all around us by day and by night, Jesus the Light of the world.
>   —George O. Elderken

Jesus is our hope. He was a man in whose mouth there was no guile, and in whose heart sin found no place. Even His enemies never produced any trustworthy evidence against Him. Jesus, our hope, was a conqueror who has never bowed His knees under the sway of Baal. Never stooped to the lust of power. Never worshiped the god of greed.

Jesus, our hope, endured human suffering and the insults of men, but still radiated the light of love. None of His time was spent avenging His hurts, or punishing His enemies. The community called the church, that He established, did not require a sword and did not need the standing armies of destruction, or any power to bring death to those who hated Him. Jesus said: "I am not come to destroy, but to fulfill" (Matt. 5:17).

Jesus taught love and not the hate that creates the grim specter of battlefields, and woes of the bereaved, the groans of the dying, and the mangled forms of the dead. Jesus does not condemn us because we are blind. He offers us light. Jesus, You are my hope! You took delight in lifting burdens from the needy. You came to save the lost! How well Edward Mote put it:

> My hope is built on nothing less
> Than Jesus' blood and righteousness;
> I dare not trust the sweetest frame,
> But wholly lean on Jesus' name.

When darkness seems to hide His face
I rest on His unchanging grace;
In ev'ry high and stormy gale,
My anchor holds within the veil.

His oath, His covenant, His blood
Support me in the whelming flood;
When all around my soul gives way,
He then is all my hope and stay.

On Christ the solid Rock I stand,
All other ground is sinking sand,
All other ground is sinking sand.

—Sermon by *J. Alfred Smith, Sr.*

2
A Pastor's Tithing Testimony

Malachi 3:8-10

If a Jew gave one tenth under the law, for a Christian to give less under grace is a disgrace! Giving is, therefore, a necessary part of Christian living. Percentage giving then enables you and me to move up the giving ladder year after year, until we have at least become as the good Jew who gave the tithe.

Too many of us are like old Deacon Horner, who sat in the corner, as the contribution box passed by. Sweetly content, he dropped in a cent, and said "what a good churchman am I." We American Christians are distracted because God has given us so much, and we have given Him so little in return.

America makes up only 6 percent of the world's population. We possess 20 percent of its gold, 40 percent of its silver, 50 percent of its zinc, 60 percent of its copper, 66 percent of its oil, 40 percent of its railroads, and 85 percent of its automobiles. Yet we disgrace our Christian boasting when we give less than 10 percent which God commands and demands. Let me tell you why I plan to continue obeying Malachi 3:8-10 by tithing.

From a negative viewpoint I tithe not because I have a surplus of money, not because I am out of debt, not because I fear that I will go to hell if I don't tithe. It is not primarily because of a sense of duty, even though I feel I have a responsibility of love that requires that I give a tithe as a minimum.

From a positive viewpoint:

I Tithe to God Through My Church to Acknowledge
Divine Ownership of All Things I Am and Have

I believe with the psalmist that "The earth is the Lord's and the fullness thereof, the world, and they that dwell therein" (Ps. 24:1).

The Lord is our creation Sustainer. As owner, He has a right to an increase from that which belongs to Him. He has clearly stated what His minimum share should be: "And all the tithe of the land, whether of the seed of the land, or of the fruit of the tree, is the Lord's: it is holy unto the Lord" (Lev. 27:30).

The law asks for only 10 percent. The hotel-restaurant industry asks for a 15 percent gratuity. The prophet Malachi is even more candid by stating the amount which belongs to God. We must beware lest we labor under the impression that if we give the tithe, we have met our financial obligation to God. Malachi 3:8 reads: "Will a man rob God? Surely not! And yet you have robbed me. 'What do you mean? When did we ever rob you?' You have robbed me of tithes and offerings due to me" (TLB).

The Bible says tithes come first—then the offerings. Offerings are like icing on the cake. Some of us give the icing without the cake, and still some of us give the cake without the icing.

I Tithe to God Through My Church Because the Tithe
Is God's Method for Financing His Kingdom

A. Our Lord gave His church a commission which is worldwide in its significance (Matt. 28:18-20).

B. In writing to the church at Corinth, Paul made specific reference to the fact that their offerings should be proportionate (1 Cor. 16:2). In no verse of Scripture is it even suggested that God's people should give less than 10 percent of their increase for the Lord's work.

I Tithe to God Through the Church
Because I Want to Be Honest

A. I want to be honest in all my business relationships.

B. Most of all, I want to be honest with God. If the tithe belongs to God, I want Him to have every cent of it. I do not believe I can prosper by withholding from God that which belongs to Him.

I Tithe to God Through My Church Because it Helps Me to Be More Christlike

A. A Christian is one who is like Christ. Christ is the One who gave Himself unselfishly for us.

To buy us out of the slave markets of sin, Jesus left the riches of heaven and took upon Himself the poverty of earth that you and I could become heirs to the riches of eternal life. Jesus came from the halls of heaven to the nails of the cross; from heaven's commendations to earth's condemnation; from heaven's honors to Calvary's horrors. What a price for Jesus to pay! He didn't have to do it, but thank God He did!

The law of heaven is love because God is love. My giving to God is an expression of my love to God, who so loved me that He gave His Son to die for me. The law of earth is selfishness. All of us have an inward inclination toward selfishness. We are taught to get all we can, and to can all we get. It is easy to believe that a man's life consists of the abundance of the things which he possesses. The world encourages us to measure success in terms of the things we acquire. God measures us in terms of what we give, and the manner in which we give.

I Tithe to God Through the Church Because I Desire the Blessings God Has Promised the Tither

A part of the blessing of God to the tither comes in a satisfied conscience. I can feel good in knowing that I obeyed my Heavenly Father. A part of the blessing of God to the tither is knowing that through giving, we make evangelism and missions possible. We have made the best possible investment when we tithe.

Conclusion

I pay a tithe and bring an offering to the church, not to try to pay God for His blessings, but so I can say, "Thank You, Lord," by giving generously to Christ. I say, "Thank You, Lord," for your countless blessings.

"Thank You, Lord," for sweet communion, for pardon, for Your presence, for Your power. "Thank You, Lord," for providing all of my needs. "Thank You, Lord," for allowing me to serve You as a Christian steward. Most of all, thank You, Lord, for Jesus Christ, my Redeemer.

> Oh God, we pray for security and more for courage to do Your will. Help us to cherish as friends, not those who make us uncomfortable, but those who join us in the fight for truth and justice. Teach us to honor Thee, not only with our voices, but with our lives and our pocketbooks. Send us a doing, acting, giving set of officers and followers in our church. In Jesus' Name I pray, Amen.

JAS, Sr.

3
Generosity and Her Critics

Matthew 26:6-13

Generosity speaks! Listen to her:

"I invite you to journey with me backward into time. Purchase your ticket with your powers of concentration, and ride your vehicle of imagination backward past the modern era, the Middle Ages, the Christian era, into the biblical world of Jesus.

"Things look very different. We see men and women dressed in similar clothing. All of the men wear long gowns, most have beards, a few wear turbans, and practically all of them, with the exception of a few bald ones, have long hair.

"Children can be heard playing in the narrow streets of crowded Jerusalem. The marketplace is jammed with women carrying water pots and food baskets on their heads. Camels kneel down to be watered, and the bleating of sheep can be heard above the braying of the donkeys.

"As we move rapidly out of Jerusalem, I can't help recalling the criticism and cross-examination of hostile witnesses and the suffering that occurred there, but I see a "new Jerusalem, which cometh down out of heaven from my God (Rev. 3:12b).

"We now travel eastward into the countryside for one and five-eighths of a mile into the suburban village of Bethany. In this small, quiet town we pick up the strong scent of almond trees in blossom. This fragrance mingles in the wind with the odor of the olive groves. Searching for the house of Simon the Leper, we ask a Jewish boy eating dried figs if he would assist us. He tells us to follow the crowd in front of us, and we obey. When we reach Simon's house he welcomes us, but he forgets to wash our feet (most hosts generally wash their guests' feet). Sandal wearing on hot, dusty soil makes the feet tender. A guest asks us not to become upset since Simon forgot to wash the feet of Jesus, the guest of honor. We look around the room, and Jesus is seated at the center of the table. Jesus, you see, is the center of attraction. Old religious leaders called Pharisees are watching Jesus with others—poorer people who survive through cooperation and interdependence.

"These are the people who know me best. I have noticed when people really come to know me, they feel they don't need anything, or anyone else. When I become their friend, they feel they don't even need God. When I'm there, people feel everyone wants to be around them. They find it hard really to trust others because they think others want to take me away from them. Honestly speaking, I have noticed most people don't even know how to treat me, or what to do with me when I am around! Sometimes when I'm out trying to share myself with others, there are those who beg for more and more of me, until sometimes they find themselves in so far over their heads. They tear down their barns and build bigger ones for me to live in. I have given them peace, health, love, and long life. I have been extremely kindhearted and noble. I have brought some people bountiful blessings too numerous to count. Even in their sins I have made promises to them who were willing to turn from their wicked ways. I have lived up to my name, I believe.

"Those of you who have wrong values and a harmful philosophy of economics, who try to keep up with the Joneses by obtaining as much of my wares as possible, who—when you feel you have accumulated as much of me as the Joneses—want to boast about me and show me off, have distributed me to the butcher, the banker, and the BMW maker, and there's none of me left to share with God. Truly I say, wherever the gospel is preached in the whole world, what I have done for you will be in memory of Jesus Christ. We have taken a look at me. Now let us examine my critics.

"I don't know why I, Generosity, and my twin sister, Kindness, are always the objects of criticism. Those who talked evil about Jesus and who planned His death were left unnoticed and untouched, but I was put down when I tried to show my love for the Master. What's even worse is that my critics were good people.

"They were the disciples of the Lord who should have known better, disciples whom I had befriended—Peter, James, John, and others, whose ministries I had anointed. How could the disciples be for Jesus and at the same time be against me? How could the disciples know that Jesus needed love, yet criticize me when I showed up as a woman and offered expensive perfume to Jesus? Why did they want to deny Jesus the extravagance of my gift? By criticizing me, the disciples exposed their own spiritual immaturity. Just as you modern people criticize your family members for their generosity of time, tithes, and talents toward the Word of Jesus Christ, you expose your spiritual immaturity because:

"1. You reveal your lack of confidence in God's Word. God's Word says He will open up the windows of heaven and pour generosity on you!

"Try me.

"2. You show immaturity when you take the spotlight of truth off your own shortcomings and criticize someone who is loving God with their generosity.

"I am an act of love. No one can tell another when he or she has loved too much or has gone too far. Sometimes Satan will dispatch one of his angels, who will whisper into the ear of one of God's saints, "You are doing too much, slow down, don't let them use you like that." Love has no limits if it is true love. True love goes as far as it can go. Unlimited love is often rejected because people are afraid of true, unlimited, unconditional, and bona fide love.

"Look at the disciples in this text. They criticized the woman because of her unlimited love for Jesus. Why? Because they didn't want to go all the way to Calvary with Jesus. They left Jesus in the garden. Jesus wants me to tell my story! He wants the preachers to tell my story. He wanted the woman to tell my story, which is also her story. He wants my story to be your story. What are you willing to give to Jesus? While others are thinking of financial advantage and economic profit, when others are sitting in the seat of the scornful, with their minds in the mood of self-righteous judgment, and their spirits in the attitude of sour nonsympathy, I gave Jesus my best. Jesus said, 'She anointed me for my death and burial. Her act which to you seemed to be a great waste, was my greatest human gift' (Matt. 26:12, Author).

"Wherever the Christian gospel is preached, you will hear about me. Jesus said that my story will be told as a memorial. Wherever, yes wherever; it in the straw-roofed huts of Africa, in the icy plains of Greenland, in the humming-buzzing cities of Europe and America, in the rich agricultural lands of middle America, in the prosperous comfort and well-manicured and beautifully cultivated communities of the suburbs, wherever, yes wherever. Even in the disadvantaged, poverty-laden areas of the inner city, or in the cold, barren, cell blocks of city jails and federal prisons, on the front porch of Grandmama's cottage, if the gospel is preached, my story will be told! What is my name? Well, my friends call me Gene, others call me Generosity, but my name is not important."

JAS, Sr.

4
God's Poverty, Our Riches

> For ye know the grace of our Lord Jesus Christ, that, though he was rich, yet for your sakes he became poor, that ye through his poverty might be rich (2 Cor. 8:9).

In his second letter to the church at Corinth, the apostle Paul put heavy emphasis on the word *grace*. This word is seldom used today. In fact, the only time we hear the word is in the church, or when we meet someone by the name of Grace. What does this mean? How would you explain it to a non-Christian?

T. DeWitt Jowett gave an excellent definition of grace:

> Grace is divine energy. Grace is divine energy of holiness. Grace is divine energy of holiness issuing in the ministry of love. Grace is divine energy issuing in the ministry of love in quest of the unlovely. Grace is divine energy of love issuing in the ministry of love in quest of the unlovely, and by communication of itself, converting the unlovely into loveliness. Grace is the holy love of God in quest of un- lovely man, seeking to woo and win, and transfigure him into the loveliness of the Lord Jesus Christ.

I added to Dr. Jowett's definition the fact that grace is not duty. *Duty* brings Christians to church because Christians ought to at- tend. *Love* brings you to church because you enjoy coming, but grace is love plus the divine pull of Jesus Christ. Grace is love outdoing itself.

> Love turns toward the lovable,
> Grace to the undeserving.

> Love often looks upward,
> Grace always looks downward.
> Love looks out for excellency,
> Grace looks out for sin.
> Love discovers merit,
> Grace creates it.
> Love has to be evoked,
> Grace acts of its own accord.
> Love is involuntary,
> Grace always takes the initiative.
>
> —Author unknown

What is grace, you ask? I answer, grace is love beyond the bounds of love—love, outloving love, love loving where there is no ground to justify the loving, the infinite coming in touch with the finite; majesty with meanness; and stainless purity coming into contact with the sins of mankind, like the snow of heaven with the mire and slush of the street. This is what Paul meant when he wrote: "For ye know the grace of our Lord Jesus Christ" (2 Cor. 8:9).

Well, Paul, what about "the grace of our Lord Jesus Christ?" Hear Paul answering: "Though he was rich, yet for our sakes he became poor."

Look at Jesus full of grace and truth. All the way from heaven to earth He stoops, from glory to gloom He leaps, from paradise to persecution, and from life to death He springs. He descends from the highest throne to the cruelest cross. He gives up heaven's riches for earth's poverty.

"Though he was rich, yet for your sakes he became poor."—Let us for a moment open the curtains of eternity, and gaze on the stupendous wealth of the Christ. The Bible tells us that Jesus Christ, the Eternal Word, is the Maker of the universe. Listen to God's written Word:

> "In the beginning was the Word, and the Word was with God, and the Word was God.... All things were made by him; and without him was not anything made that was made" (John 1:1,3).

All the precious gems and rich metals that ever sparkled are His. He made them. This world, with all its majestic, sun-kissed mountains, broad oceans, winding rivers, babbling brooks, laughing valleys, and sparkling fountains are His.

The cattle on ten thousand hills were created by Jesus Christ, who confuses our intellect and destroys our human logic, causing us to accept Him through faith, since in His eternal nature, He invaded time, as a baby older than His mother. This mysteriously powerful God said in the Book of Genesis: "Let there be" (1:3,6,9,11,14), and *creation* trickled from His fingers like pearly dewdrops from the rosy fingers of the morning.

In the richness of eternity, the Bible in the Book of Hebrews said, "[Jesus was] the brightness of his glory, and the express image of his person" (1:3). The Book of Revelation says, "His hairs were white like wool [this eternal Christ had] feet like unto fine brass, as if they burned in a furnace; and his voice as the sound of many waters" (Rev. 1:14-15). No wonder the human Christ, before going to die on the cross, prayed in John's Gospel: "And now O Father, glorify thou me . . . with the glory I had with thee before the world was" (17:5).

"Though he was rich. . . ." Rich in material possessions, rich in the glory of God, rich in the majesty of a king. Isaiah the court prophet, the most adept and cultured of all the prophets of God, wrote: "I saw also the Lord, sitting upon a throne, high and lifted up, and his train filled the temple" (Isa. 6:1).

Though he was rich in honor. The Book of Revelation says: "[salvation], and honor, and glory, and power, be unto [our God] that sitteth upon the throne" (5:13).

"Though he was rich, yet for your sakes he became poor."—

Jesus Was Born Poor, Lived Poor, and Died Poor

The earth gave Him a chilling reception upon His birth, and heaven dispatched an angelic choir to echo through the skies the anthem: "Glory to God in the highest, and on earth peace, good will toward men" (Luke 2:14).

While heaven honored baby Jesus, the earth did not blow a trumpet, wave a flag, or burn a torch in recognition of His birth. Earth receives her princes and presidents amid the shouts of the people and the strains of music, but the best door opened for Jesus was a barn door. The best bed, a litter of straw; the best cradle, a manger. Born in a stable of poverty, rocked in a cradle of poverty, lulled to sleep in the arms of the mother from Nazareth, a city noted for its poverty. Many times the rocks on the mountainsides were His only pillows, and the blue canopy of heaven His only covering. Jesus said, "The foxes have holes, the birds of the air have nests; but the Son of man hath not where to lay his head" (Matt. 8:20).

To our knowledge Jesus rode only once, and that was on a borrowed beast. The boat on which He taught was a borrowed boat. He wrought a miracle to obtain money to pay His taxes. His grave was a borrowed tomb. Instead of the nectar of heaven, the earth gave Him vinegar to drink, a reed for a scepter, thorns for a crown, and a cross for a throne.

Jesus was poor. "For ye know the grace of our Lord Jesus Christ, that though he was rich, yet for your sakes he became poor" (2 Cor. 8:9). Jesus was poor in the eyes of the world. He trod the winepress alone. Hence, the world called Jesus "sabbath breaker, winebibber, traitor, friend of sinners, and blasphemer." He who owned everything, owned nothing. He whom heaven honored, was rejected by earth, dying in shame, forsaken by His disciples, and so heartbroken that one of His seven last words from Calvary's cross was: "My God, my God, why hast thou forsaken me?" (Mark 16:34).

A songwriter said He didn't have to do it. Well, why did He do it? Was it simply to please the Father? No, He had already done that. At Jesus' baptism a voice from heaven said: "This is my beloved Son, in whom I am well pleased" (Matt. 3:17). It was not to increase His own glory. He was great enough. He already had supreme power. At His feet rolled seas of glory and on His brow perched the eternal fame of heaven. He was King of kings. To Him gold was sordid dust and jewels were gaudy toys. He did it. Yes,

He did become poor that we through His poverty might become rich.

Christians, People Who Know Christ, Are Rich

Christians have in Jesus Christ wealth incorruptible, inexhaustible, and unsearchable.

Let us argue this point more clearly to see if I am right. Though you and I may have little money, in Christ we have the riches of God's forgiveness, the wealth of God's peace that passeth human understanding. Moreover, as Christians, we have the wealth of eternal salvation. In his Ephesian letter Paul put it this way. We have: (1) the riches of saints in Christ Jesus, and (2) the riches of Christ Jesus in the saints. This thought of Paul's says two things: (1) The source of Christian riches is in the Christ who became poor so we could enjoy heaven's riches; and (2) We are the rich possessions of Jesus Christ. Jesus has put His value on us. In our own eyes we may not see ourselves as persons of worth, persons of value. But in His eyes He has called us His riches. He valued us enough to die for us. The value of land is not in the amount of dirt that makes up the land. The value in the land is in how much the buyer will pay for it. When we were on the slave auction block of sin, the devil wanted to buy us, but his bid was too low. Jesus purchased our salvation by paying the highest price. He paid for us with His blood.

I am rich today! I am rich because God numbered me with Paul, Apollos, and Cephas to preach the unsearchable riches of Christ Jesus. I can warn, instruct, rebuke, and point people to the Lamb of God that taketh away the sins of the world, who gives the bread of heaven and the water of life. In His name I cheer those who are in the valley of the shadow of death. In His name I visit the sick. In his name I bury the dead and give hope to the despairing! In His name I tell Christians about 39,000 promises of the Bible that inform us that eternity with Christ is far better than time and eternity without Him.

If you don't know Him confess your sins, and come to Him now.

If you haven't met Jesus, turn your back on the world, and come to Him now.

If you will, at this moment, invite God into your heart.

JAS, Sr.

5

The War on Debt

"The borrower is servant to the lender" (Prov. 22:7).
"Go to the ant, thou sluggard; consider her ways and be wise" (Prov. 6:6).

Introduction

The amount of money the average family owes to banks, department stores, and other lending institutions has risen every year for the past thirty years. Consumer debt has increased at a higher rate than the cost of living. The debt of the average family represents a much larger percentage of the average earnings of working family members.

Thirty years ago only about 10 percent of individual earnings was spent on consumer debt. Today that figure has risen to a staggering 19 percent. That means almost one-fifth of the average person's earnings is now spent to service his ever-increasing debt.

American consumer debt grew by almost $50 billion in 1988. This brought the total to about $700 billion. This means that if the present debt were to be evenly divided among every man, woman, and child in the United States, they would each owe about $2,800. This consumer debt does not include the more than $1 trillion ($1,000 billion) that the American public owes to various lending institutions on their home mortgages.

The debt problem is further aggravated by a generation of persons addicted to credit card debt. Just as there are people who are junk food junkies, who cannot control their appetites for unhealthy foods, so are there financial junkies who cannot control their appetite for compulsive buying.

Hidden Debt

Compulsive spending and compulsive credit card charging are separate and apart from hidden debt. Taxes constitute hidden debt. The average American had to work 124 days in 1990, a whopping 34 percent of the year, just to pay his/her federal, state, and local taxes. Looking at it from a monthly perspective, you have to work four full months of the year just to pay your taxes. In 1989 the average American had worked since January 1 in order to earn enough money to pay his/her tax debt off on "Tax Freedom Day" (April 15). Looking at it on a daily basis, the average worker toiled two hours and forty-three minutes out of every eight-hour day to satisfy his 1989 tax debt. This means that every day you had to work two hours and forty-three minutes for the government before you started earning any money for yourself. The federal government collected $1.07 trillion in revenue in 1990. That's up $86 billion from 1989. Yet the Congressional Budget Office predicted a deficit of $155 billion. On an average, the national debt grows at the rate of $722 million per day. If you had all of your own personal debts paid off, and if you did not owe anybody anything, your personal share of our federal government debt would be $11,209.54. Add this amount for each member of your family in order to determine your entire family's share of our federal government debt.

Attention has been given to discussing consumer debt, the debt of the federal government, and hidden debt. Please allow me to focus more specifically upon personal debt.

Personal Debt

The average Christian spends 34 percent of his or her wages to pay Caesar or the government while spending less than 2 percent on all Christian endeavors combined. Why is this? This is because the creditor is at the Christian's door. The mortgage is due. There is nowhere to hide. The Christian is a slave to his or her money. The Christian could tithe, instead of tipping God, if the Christian were not a slave to money. Money should serve the Christian, not enslave the Christian.

The Christian brings up the family in a house with a thirty-year mortgage. The Christian drives an automobile with a five-year loan. The Christian buys new clothes with plastic credit cards that charge as high as 21 percent interest per year. The Christian sleeps on a mortgaged bed, sits on mortgaged furniture, and watches color television on a set which will hopefully be paid off before it breaks down. Vacations are paid for with convenient monthly payments. The Christian ends up owing his or her soul to the god of personal debt. Instead of working for God, the Christian works for the god of personal debt.

Take a look at yourself. Ask yourself: "Am I working for the god of personal debt?" You say, "How would I know if I am a slave to personal debt?" Here is how you can know if you are working for the god of personal debt.

1. You are in trouble when you pay more than 20 percent of your gross income on consumer debt. That includes credit card purchases, personal and student loans, not including your house payment or rent.

2. You are in trouble when you can only afford to pay the minimum monthly payments on your credit card debt.

3. You are in trouble when you start taking those preapproved credit cards because you have exhausted the current ones you already have.

4. You are in trouble when you use credit cards to pay the minimum payment for other credit cards.

5. You are in trouble when you rob Peter to pay Paul. This month you miss your student loan payment to pay your department store's clothing account and try to catch up next month. You will never catch up. You will get farther behind with the interest that you have to pay on the unpaid balance and on the late charges. This means double interest payments on the loan.

6. You are in trouble when you try to borrow your way out of debt. You can't borrow your way out of debt. You pay your way out of debt.

7. You are in trouble spiritually when The Great Commission becomes The Great Omission. God has told you to take the gospel to the whole world. You can't give tithes and offerings to extend the gospel in your city, in your nation, and around the world because you have overextended yourself in debt.

8. You are in trouble because you are an emotional buyer who does not shop for the best price. You are in trouble because you do not shop for the best loan with the best interest rates. Well, preacher, since I am in trouble, please tell me how I can get out of trouble.

How to Get Out of Trouble

Preacher, I am in trouble. I have allowed money to be my master and not my servant. I am a prisoner of overextended credit. I have anxiety, worry, and no peace of mind. Bad debts cause me and my wife to quarrel, and bad debts have broken my friendships.

As a preacher of good news, I ask you to read your Bible:

1. *Read Genesis 18:14*—"Is anything too hard for the Lord?" Believe that if you obey the Scriptures, God will help you with your debt problem.
2. *Read Luke 12:22-23*—"Jesus said . . . Life is much more important than food and the body much more important than clothes" (GNB).
3. *Read Proverbs 6:6-7*—"Lazy people should learn a lesson from the way ants live. They have no leader, chief, or ruler, but they store up their food during the summer, getting ready for winter" (GNB).

Proverbs 6:6 says: "Go to the ant, thou sluggard; consider her ways and be wise."

1. The ant works patiently.
2. The ant works progressively.
3. The ant works presently for the future.

Proverbs 30:25 tells us "ants are creatures of little strength" (NIV). Black people are creatures of little strength like ants. But if black people would use ant sense, and work together, and save their money together, then we could say to them, as Proverbs 30:25 says of ants: "Ants are creatures of little strength, yet they store up their food in the summer."

Ants survive in summer and winter, in good times and bad times. Ants do not survive through greedy, selfish, competitive, individualistic efforts. Ants collectivize and harmonize their efforts for common, economic survival. When ants come together, elephants cannot run them out of the forest.

Teach us, Lord, to develop the economic unity of ants. Teach us to remember how Jesus canceled our sin debt in order to purchase for us eternal life.

JAS, Sr.

6
Righteous Misgiving About Unrighteous Giving

Luke 11:42

The first part of my message is parabolic. Jesus taught people by parables because He knew that what they saw stayed with them longer than what they heard or even what they read. One of our church members, Roy Combs, was twenty-six when he started practicing law. I knew him when he was born. His family and our family are very close. Brother Combs is not only making a contribution as a young attorney, but he is giving his time to help young people make it. He does not feel that because the Lord is blessing him he should simply boast, "I have it made." He has a ladder, and he is trying to pull people up. We can see that not all of our young people are on the wrong road, can't we? He is recruiting tutors to work with him at the local Street Academy.

As you are aware, you can't even be in the military unless you can operate computers these days. Even the military doesn't want you if you don't have an education. So the only way our people will make it will be to receive some training.

Also in our church is Judge Allen Broussard, who started practicing in this town at the age of twenty-six, and now he is retired. The point is that when one steps down he should be able to pass the baton on. That's a beautiful picture. One man is starting out at age twenty-six. Another has gone as high as a judge in the California Supreme Court. Judge Broussard is retired and is perhaps the only judge on the bench who understands the hurt and pain of the little person down at the bottom. He has fought persistently to see that we obtain justice. I've learned by experience that when I have an opportunity to do good, not to talk about it. Just go on and do it, and the Lord will reward you. Talking about things like that just increases the jealousy and attacks that people will make on you.

Allen Temple has honored Judge Broussard with a plaque which reads, "Allen Temple Baptist Church honors California Supreme Court Justice Allen Broussard for outstanding judicial leadership as an African American serving on the highest court in this State and a positive role model for black youths and adults. Allen Temple Baptist Church, Oakland, California."

I would like for you to repeat after me, "How terrible for you Pharisees. You give to God one tenth of the seasoning herbs, such as mint and rue and all the other herbs, but you neglect justice, and love for God. These you should practice without neglecting the others" (Luke 11:42, GNB). This is the text for this message.

Many Christians have a strong passion for understanding the Scriptures. They are serious about perceiving and obeying the teachings of Jesus Christ. They become discouraged when the teachings of the Old and New testaments appear to disagree. In a motivation revival at Pilgrim Hope Baptist Church of Los Angeles, California, this issue was brought to my attention. One night I preached on the topic, "I Am Your Offering Envelope." It was based on 1 Corinthians 16:1-4. After preaching that sermon I received, that same night, a letter from a member of the church.

The letter began: "Pastor Smith, in your teaching this week could you please bring the Old Testament Scripture, Malachi 3:10, into focus for those of us who choose to ignore the fact that it is still God's law? We need to be edified on the desires God has for us. God bless you." Immediately I asked God to provide me with helpful answers to this sincere and intelligent question. All of my childhood days in my home church in Kansas City, Missouri, with Pilgrim Rest Baptist Church, I had heard people say that we are under Jesus Christ and not under Moses. Therefore, they claimed, since we are New Testament Christians under grace and not under the law of Moses, tithing is obsolete for modern Christians. And here I was facing this argument in Los Angeles as an adult. What answer would I give?

The member who had written the letter asked, "Pastor, while you are here with us this week, clear up the matter." Well, I was taught that the Old Testament was Jesus Christ concealed and that the New Testament was Jesus Christ revealed. So the New Testament helps us understand Old Testament teachings on tithing. I was also taught that Jesus was the authority for my beliefs and not Moses; that Jesus was the authority for my beliefs and not tradition; that Jesus was the authority for my beliefs and not my personal feelings. I was also taught that tithing in the Old Testament was older than Moses. Jesus is the "I AM" of both the Old and New testaments.

Do you know what I mean when I say He is the "I AM" of the Old Testament? When Moses stood at the burning bush he asked God, "What's your name?" and God replied, "I AM that I AM" (Ex. 3:14). And when Jesus stood in the New Testament Gospel of John, they asked who He was, and He declared, "I AM. I am the Bread of Life. I am the true Vine. I am the Good Shepherd. I am the Water of Life. I am the resurrection and the life." So if Jesus is the I AM of the Old Testament and the Old Testament—"In the beginning God" (that's how Genesis starts), and the New Testament, "In the beginning was the Word" (that's how the Gospel of John starts)—then you and I have no alternative but to hear what Jesus has to say about tithing.

In New Testament Scripture, Matthew 5:17, Jesus said, "Think not that I am come to destroy the law, or the prophets: I am not come to destroy, but to fulfill." In Luke 11:42, in reference to tithing, Jesus told the Pharisees, "for ye tithe mint and rue and all manner of herbs, and pass over judgment and justice and the love of God: these ought ye to have done, and not to leave the other undone." These you ought to have done, tithing, but you have left the other, justice and the love of God, undone. The real issue is not how we feel about it, what we are in the habit of doing, what we have learned from tradition, or what we see the majority of the people around us doing. That's not the real issue. The real issue is do we choose to obey Jesus Christ? The real issue is not what Pastor Smith teaches, but what Jesus teaches about the issue. The issue is not whether we want to debate between the teachings of the Old and the New testaments. In fact, the Old Testament starts with easy stewardship, and the New Testament leads us into sacrificial stewardship.

That was my immediate reaction to the question from a sensitive, intelligent student of Scripture in Los Angeles. Now allow me to reveal to you, as best I can, the deeper truths I discovered from a careful and prayerful examination of our text. Deeper discovery of Luke 11:42 helped me to see that Jesus had righteous misgiving about unrighteous giving. Unrighteous giving can be practiced by those who tithe and those who do not tithe. Unrighteous giving can be practiced by both the pulpit and the pew.

What is unrighteous giving? Tell me, preacher, when is giving unrighteous? Tell me, Pastor Smith, is the teaching portion of this message how tithers and nontithers both can practice unrighteous giving? Giving is unrighteous when it is legalistic. Giving is unrighteous when it is simply doing your duty or paying your dues. Some people will say "I pay my lodge dues"; "I pay my sorority dues"; "I pay my church dues." But I want you to remember that you cannot pay your dues to God. The cost is too high. How could you pay for just one beat of your heart? The cost is too high, I tell you.

The fact is that you and I both are imperfect, and God has to forgive us every day. You can't pay any dues. Salvation is not by works. You don't have enough money to pay God what He deserves. You are not doing God a favor by going to church. But God has done you a favor by allowing your sins to be under His blood. So when you put your money in whether you are a tither or a nontither, your giving is unrighteous if you are legalistic, and you feel you are merely doing your duty. "I paid my dues this Sunday. I have as much right as anybody else to have my say around here." No, you don't. You're here by the grace of God—amazing grace, amazing because God gives it back to us over and over again, whether or not we deserve it. It's amazing because when God prepares to bless you, nobody can stop Him from doing it.

Giving is unrighteous when it is simply an income-tax shelter from the Internal Revenue Service. I've seen some of our members not giving a cent during the year, but then they visit their accountant, who says, "Look, you could've saved giving to Uncle Sam if you would've given more to charity or to the church." Then they run into the church with a big check at the last minute. We are always thrilled to receive the money because our church always needs it. Our missionaries need to be paid every month; we need gasoline for the church bus; lights have to be paid every month. And you should not—if you sing "Oh, how I love Jesus, Oh, how I love Jesus, Oh, how I love Jesus, Because He first loved me"—give because you're giving as a mere income-tax shelter. The gift is good but the motive is selfish, and when the motive is selfish, giving is unrighteous.

Giving is unrighteous when it is an outward display for publicity or an expression of power within the political structure of the church. I want to make this point, so repeat it after me? "Giving is unrighteous when it is an outward display for publicity or an expression of power within the political structure of the church." "What are you talking about, Pastor Smith? Unpack that. Money talks; money gives me political control in my church. My withholding of large gifts to my church can be an expression of political control or my personal dissatisfaction." Did you all read Luke 21:1-4, where Jesus condemns such behavior?

Giving is unrighteous when it uses the tithes as the basis for not giving offerings. "Pastor Smith, is this your opinion?" No, in a way I wish it were my opinion, but I did not make this statement. Malachi 3 speaks of tithes *and* offerings. Tithing is not the ceiling for giving. According to the Scripture, tithing is the floor where Christians should begin their acts of giving. If you begin with your tithes, then you move beyond tithes to what? That's what the Scripture says. Unrighteous giving says "only 10 percent belongs to God. God does not care if I gamble with my 90 percent. God does not care if I drink it up with my 90 percent. God does not care if I buy crack and cocaine with the 90 percent." There are folks who believe that if I give God 10 percent I can spend 20 percent at the racetrack. This is not popular preaching, but it is the truth.

I went to a restaurant the other day and pulled out a little card called the "tip card." My tip table indicates that if the check is $20, the tip if $3. If the check is $49, the tip is $7.35, because you are supposed to give 15 percent. I pulled out my tip table and prepared to figure in my tip so I could use it for income-tax deductions because it was a business lunch. But the Lord said, "Since you're so smart, you'd better look at that bill." I looked again, and they had increased the amount of the gratuity. They want a gratuity of 15 percent or more.

If you go to an athletic contest you are going to buy the ticket, pay for the gas to travel there, and lay out money for parking and concessions. The point I am trying to make is that giving is unrighteous if you give your tithes and then claim you can do what you want to with the 90 percent. Jesus Christ wants to be the Lord of *all* of your lives. He's not simply interested in being Lord of the Sunday segment. Somehow I fall into trouble if I preach a little bit longer and go overtime, but the ball player has no trouble if he has to carry the game into overtime. So we have to examine our priorities. In our church we have to ask ourselves, "Is this the Allen Temple Society, or is this the Allen Temple Baptist Church that believes in one Lord, one faith, and one baptism?"

Let me give you the good news. The gospel has bad news first, and then it has good news second. "The wages of sin is death" (Rom 6:23a). That's bad news. The good news is, "but the gift of God is eternal life through Jesus Christ our Lord" (Rom. 6:23b). Will you help us look at ourselves as individuals? Not the pastor, not the deacons, not the trustees, not the choir, not the ministers in training, not my husband, not my wife, not my children, not my mother, not my father, but "It's me, O Lord, Standin' in the need of prayer." And if the sermon does not lead us into that kind of personal encounter with God, then the minister is not preaching the Word of God. That's the bad news. But there is good news. The good news is that we don't need to feel guilty about our sins because we have been forgiven. The Judge has acquitted us. The Judge has announced that we are free, and the Judge is a judge of not only the first chance, but the second chance, the third chance, the fourth chance, and the fifth chance. And so God advises, "Take My Word today. I've given you a new chance. I've given you a new opportunity. I've given you another day." So this new day is the first day of the rest of your life. Therefore, you can practice righteous giving.

Giving is righteous when the giver never contributes as an act of pride or self-righteousness, but always as an act of gratitude for the mercy of God. Therefore, when I bring my offering, it is my way of saying, "Lord, You didn't have to do it, but You did. Thank You, Jesus." Righteous giving occurs when the visible, giving hand is an expression of love from an invisible and sincere heart. By that I mean the visible, giving hand drops the envelope into the plate. And at the plate marked "benevolence," the deacons will have the resources to feed a hungry person that you will never meet, or help a senior citizen pay his utility bills in the winter. Your visible hand will bless some invisible person. When you do that, giving is righteous.

Righteous giving takes place when the giver gives to promote the advancement of God's cause in the world. The giver never says he is giving to the preacher. Amen. The giver never says, "I am giving to the trustees." Amen. I brought my own amens. The giver never says, "I am giving to the church." Amen. The giver never says, "I am giving to the poor." The righteous giver realizes that inasmuch as he has given to one of God's little ones, he has given to God. For in Matthew 25:34b,36b, the Lord says, "Come, ye blessed of my Father. . . . I was in prison, and ye came unto me." And then we'll ask, "Lord, when did we do that?" Yet, there were times when you could not go to San Quentin with Reverend Stephens. Reverend Stephens represents us there. Sometimes Stephens carries provisions into the prison for a Christian prisoner who has messed up and is trying to put his life back together and won't do something illegal in prison in order to make money. So when you bless a prison ministry, Jesus noted, "You have done it under Me."

I cannot buy salvation by giving money, but I can express my love for God, and I can demonstrate God's love in my heart by giving. I can give to bless God's people. I can give to promote God's work. I will give back a portion of my God-given blessing to the One who left heaven's riches and became earthly poor so I might enjoy the priceless riches of eternity. I will give. I will give because the living Christ, who gave His all, lives in me. I give not because I am so generous, but because Christ lives inside of me. Christ lives in me like a stream of water that never dries up. The sun gives. I ought to give. The flowers give. I ought to give. The clouds give. I ought to give. The sea gives. I ought to give. The earth gives. I ought to give. The birds give. I ought to give. The fish give. I ought to give. Angels give. I ought to give. Jesus gave. I ought to give.

I want to extend the invitation. "God so loved the world that He gave. . . ." The Holy Spirit tells me that Deacon Sellers ought to sing that song "God So Loved the World." That's the only way I could become a Christian—because Jesus gave.

JAS, Sr.

7

The High Cost of Bread

John 6:5-12,34-41
(Preached for the New Year 1991)

Jesus looked around and saw that a large crowd was coming to Him. "He asked Philip, 'Where can you buy enough food to feed all of these people?' (He said this to test Philip; actually he already knew what he would do.) Philip answered, 'For everyone to have even a little it will take more than two hundred silver coins to buy enough bread'" (GNB).

The new year, 1991, presents us a rather gloomy forecast. You can have an optimistic outlook of life like myself or Chairman Olen Grant, who is an advocate of positive thinking, but still you have to be able to admit, if you are going to be honest about it, that this new year presents a somewhat bleak picture. We don't have to be reminded or given any sort of analytical basis for being fearful of war. We know that every day brings us perhaps a little closer to war in the Persian Gulf. One day we feel hopeful because there are talks either by President Bush or Saddam Hussein about a peace initiative, only to find that as soon as those utterances are made there is a follow-up statement pointing to war.

We look at this year and are disturbed about the state of the African-American community. All we shared week after week, statistics and conditions, points to a sad plight. I need not elaborate on our condition as a people—simply to say that with the rise of diseases, with the problems of health maintenance, and with the burdens of poverty, violence, and crime, we are a jeopardized nation of people. Not only are we jeopardized here in the United

States, but unless attention is given to our mother land, we may see populations almost totally obliterated.

The United States has been somewhat insensitive to the threat of AIDS in the motherland. The United States has turned its back on the Sudan and other parts of Africa where people are starving now in rates that are even greater than the Ethiopian famine of several years ago. We are people in jeopardy, and this year doesn't show any signs of reversing this particular scenario. Then, when we look at our economy we are saddened even more, saddened because the administration has finally admitted that we are in a recession. For the administration to admit we are in a recession means we're probably closer to a depression. It's a sad economic forecast because we have seen Sears lay off hundreds. We have seen important businesses close down here in our area. J. C. Penney, which is only a few blocks away from us, threatens to close down. The unemployment rate has reached a new high for this particular period in the life of our state and our nation. When we look at the barometer of our economy there are several factors that could be considered. We can look at what is going on in the real estate market. We can look at what is going on with oil prices as a result of the war. We can look at the price of consumer goods.

And, my sisters and brothers, there is a particular consumer good which for centuries has served as a barometer of how the economy is doing. That consumer good is a staple we call bread. Bread has been an important staple going back to that ancient African kingdom we know as Egypt. The Egyptians, we are told, invented bread and the ovens in which to bake the bread. Since that time many of the societies and cultures of the world have based their diets on bread. Today more people are employed by bread bakers than any other food industry. In fact, 41 million pounds of bread are baked daily, and approximately $3 ½ billion are spent a year on bread. Bread is a staple. Bread is an important item in anyone's economy.

When we look back to the time of Jesus we see that there was a concern for the high cost of bread. Verse 7 of our text tells us that

Philip lamented the fact it would cost them some "two hundred silver coins to buy enough bread" to feed the multitude that gathered around. Now if I could break that down, it means it would take from six to eight months of wages to feed the multitude that was there. It had a high cost associated with it. We are all familiar with the story from which this question posed by Jesus emerged. We are aware of the story about how Jesus fed a multitude, including five thousand men and countless women and children. I'm wondering today if anybody followed after that little boy in the story and brought their lunch with them today. Brother Darnell Caldwell's son brought his. I look at that bread in the pail and am reminded that the bread the biblical boy brought was barley bread. Barley in those days was presented only by poor people. Barley bread was rather an embarrassment. So that little boy had to be poor. Yet, when Andrew asked him for his bread he gave all he had to the Master. Even with the high cost of bread, the boy freely gave bread to the Master.

In this story are some contrasting attitudes: *The attitudes of the crowd as a whole versus the attitude of this little boy.* As we look at the attitudes of the crowd we see there are some disturbing questions which we must pose. First, with the crowd of over five thousand people, you mean to tell me that nobody had any food with them but a little boy? These were Jewish people who were still somewhat nomadic in their orientation. They carried around baskets with food in them because they traveled. They could not eat just anybody's food but had to make sure the food was kosher and met the requirements of the Jewish dietary laws. The best means of making sure of that was to carry your own food with you. Where did the disciples find those twelve baskets for the scraps? Those are the baskets that people carried the food in. I believe, but could be wrong (but allow me to use a bit of license and conjecture that some folks had some food), that they were holding back. They were hoarding their food.

They looked out at the numbers assembled and exclaimed, "My goodness, if I share some of this there is not going to be any left for me." Beyond that we hear that it took about two hundred silver coins to buy some bread. Now while two hundred silver coins may be six to eight months of wages for one man, you mean to tell me out of those five thousand men they couldn't pool together enough silver to feed the multitude? The people were expecting a miracle. They were expecting Jesus Christ to step in and feed them when they had the ability to feed themselves.

Yes, that crowd, no doubt, included selfish people attempting to hoard what they had, and I believe that some of those people probably never ate barley bread. They had the ability to obtain the best bread. They were a material-minded people who believed in getting but not giving. And as we confront this new year we need to ask ourselves, "Is this the kind of relationship we have with Jesus? One of receiving everything and giving nothing?"

As you consider the question, "What does God expect of me in 1991?" could you come up with what you can commit to the Lord? Have you reached some sort of an impasse because your relationship with God is all about receiving and never about giving. What will you commit to God in 1991? Will you allow that little boy to be your role model and give your all to Jesus? The boy had the right attitude. He was able to take the little he had and give it to Jesus. He wasn't there checking out the crowd, wondering about the position this would give him on the makeup of the organization that had assembled. He was one little boy. He was there because he saw Jesus and he was willing to give his all to Him. And that's why Jesus declares in Matthew 18:3-4, "Except ye be converted, and become as little children, ye shall not enter into the kingdom of heaven." He goes on to say, "Whosoever shall humble himself, as this little child, the same is the greatest in the kingdom of heaven." If you want to be great, Jesus explained, "Be a servant." In 1991 this question is posed to us. Will we approach this year with the beautiful attitude of this boy who was willing to give all he had to Jesus for the benefit of the masses?

He didn't know if he would receive anything once he turned his lunch over to the adults. He had no idea if they would feed everybody else and kind of overlook him. I believe that the problems confronting our communities in 1991 are going to require us to step up our commitment. It will call for us to take what we have and turn it over to Jesus for the betterment of our communities. We can't be constant complainers and not contribute anything. To me the worst thing in the world is somebody who complains and makes no adjustments. Will we be like that little boy and invest in Jesus? For when we do the people of God will benefit. Will we be like the little boy who had the least, the very least, and offered it freely to the Lord?

When I look over my experiences here at Allen Temple I understand what my father means when he expresses a very special affection for the children and for the older folks. The children and the elders are probably locked in with the least resources. Most children don't have income coming in that they can control, and elders are often on fixed incomes, but the most generous people I have come in contact with are children and older people—children who race up to us and hug us in the reception line, who greet us with smiles of innocence, and elders who always seem to know what to say and what to do. There is one senior citizen in our church, a beautiful woman, who every Sunday sends up some throat logenzes to the preacher because she doesn't want the preacher's voice hurt from the exertion of preaching. I don't know who that senior may be in your life, but if you are anything like me, on Sunday morning you seek out that person. If you can't get close enough to them to shake their hand, make eye contact or smile at them. Let them know that you love them.

Our trustees have shared with us that out of our large membership, approximately two thousand people give less than $200 a year each. Even sadder about that statistic is that those who are on fixed incomes give more than $200 a year, and some who are making $60,000 to $70,000 and have expensive houses and cars are giving nothing! Now, I don't know who is giving what, and that has nothing to do with the pastor or assistant pastor's relationship with the members, because we don't know, and we don't want to know who gives what. But I think it is a sad commentary, sisters and brothers, that we have little children and elders who are proportionately giving more than those who have been blessed in a greater material fashion. What does God expect of you and me in 1991?

I'm so glad we know we must humble ourselves as children and understand that growth spiritually is an ongoing process. I asked Brother Charlie Gill how he was doing and rather than giving me the regular stock answer of "I'm doing fine," or "Everything is OK, how are you doing?" he replied, "Reverend, there is always room for growth." We need to understand that if we humble ourselves like a child, there is always room for growth. What measure of growth do you seek this year? Verse 26 makes us aware that the multitude sought Jesus only because they ate of the bread and were filled. They didn't seek Jesus because they understood His miracles or because they fathomed the sign that Jesus was manifesting. They sought Him because He offered them bread, and from the bread, the material bread, they were fed.

They followed Jesus for all the wrong reasons, and some of us in the church are here for all the wrong reasons. Why are you here today in the church? Are you here because of the social advantages of being a part of this distinguished congregation? Are you here because you are enabled to do business networking? Are you here because you seek to find a husband or a wife? Are you here because you have a welfare mentality, and you want to come merely to receive the blessings of God but not give back anything in return? The multitude did not consider that to follow Jesus there would be expectations of them. For Jesus taught, "If anyone would come after me, let him or her deny self, take up the cross, and follow me" (Matt. 16:24, author). To follow Jesus is going to involve some cross bearing. To follow Jesus means that sometimes we must forsake the easy road and walk up the rough side of the mountain. To follow Jesus means that we must be about the business of offering our bodies as living sacrifices which are wholly acceptable unto God, which is our reasonable service (see Rom. 12:1).

The people tried to force their own will on Jesus. They tried to take from His multiplication of the fishes and loaves a view which placed Him in their own definition of the Messianic personality. He would be the One who would free them from the oppression of Rome. That's how they saw Him. They saw Him as a liberator, One who would also provide for their material needs—but Jesus came not just for that. He came to liberate them in an eternal manner.

Why, sisters and brothers, do we seek Jesus today? Is it because Jesus would help us in a time of trouble? That's all right. Is it because Jesus is a rock in a weary land? That's all right. Do we seek Jesus because Jesus is a good companion? That's all right. Do we seek Jesus because we believe that if we pray He will provide us with material prosperity? I guess that's all right. Do we follow Jesus because we are sick and we know that He provides healing? Yes, that's all right, but that's not the ultimate reason to follow Jesus. And, as Jesus told them that material bread was OK but it was only temporal, and it was rather inferior to the real bread He had to offer, the crowd started murmuring, arguing, and rumbling. And we are told that even some of His followers, some of His disciples, started to grumble and began to fall off. Does our relationship with Allen Temple Church depend only on what Jesus through the church can provide us? But if we can't get our way, are we going to fall off? In the contemporary church there is still grumbling and mumbling. There are still uptight people, hot people, arguing people, castigating one another. Are you sitting in an anger spot? Are you angry at the preacher, or are you angry at the deacons or are you angry at the trustees? Are you sitting in an anger spot where you are mumbling and grumbling? What does God expect of us in 1991? We need to realize that we have a responsibility to Jesus, not a responsibility to the pulpit, not a responsibility to the auxiliaries or the boards, but a responsibility to Jesus.

What will you commit to Jesus this year? Will you believe in Him and do His will? Will you do His will in your life? Will you commit your whole life and life-style over to Him? It is easy to claim, ''I'll commit my life," but the test is in our life-styles. Can we commit our life-styles to Jesus? Can we look at our life, right now, and see a life-style that is pleasing to Jesus? There is always room for growth. Will you share your talent this year with Jesus? I don't know what your talents are, but I believe there are some people who are sitting on their laurels. I believe that out of this great assembly there are some people who are doing their share, and everybody else's share, too, while a whole bunch of other people are just sitting and saying, "Oh, Allen Temple, isn't Allen Temple taking care of business?" "That's my church." This year will you share your purse with Jesus? We are trying to evangelize. We are trying to go into the prisons. We are trying to reach children around here. We are trying to touch new lives for Jesus. Will you commit your purse to that? Will you commit your time? It's not enough to come here on Sunday mornings and say amen. Will you commit your time to Jesus?

As we move toward the communion table, let us be mindful that we need to be elevated above cheap grace. Dietrich Bonhoeffer said, "Cheap grace is the preaching of forgiveness without requiring repentance. Baptism without church discipline, communion without confession, absolution without personal confession." Cheap grace is grace without discipleship. It's grace without the cross, grace without Jesus Christ living and incarnate. Costly grace is the treasure hidden in a field. For the sake of it a man will gladly go and sell all he has. It is the pearl of great price which the merchant will sell all his goods to buy. It is the kingly rule of Christ for whose sake a man will pluck out the eye which causes him to stumble. It is the call of Jesus Christ at which the disciple leaves his nets and follows Him. Costliness graces the gospel—the gift which must be asked for, the door on which a person must knock. Such grace is costly because it calls us to follow Jesus Christ. It is costly because it cost a Man His life, and it is grace because it gives men, women, and children the only true life. It is costly because it condemns sin and grace because it justifies the sinner.

Above all, it is costly because it cost God the life of His Son. He was bought at a price and what has cost God much cannot be cheap for us. Above all, it is grace because God did not reckon His Son too big a price to pay for our lives but delivered Him up for us. Costly grace is the incarnation of God. God expects us to be partakers of costly grace this year. Will you pay the high cost of the bread? Will you receive Jesus Christ fully into your life this year?

The bread Jesus talks about, the bread that He offers, is not the material bread that was in the boy's lunch basket, but it's a bread that never becomes stale, never molds, never hardens, never rots. Yes, I like that physical bread, but one day there is going to be no more eating of our daily bread. One day there is going to be no more sickness. While I love Jesus, the Healer, in eternity I won't need Him as my Healer, and I'm not going to need Jesus as my Burden Bearer, because there won't be any more sickness or burdens to bear. One day in His kingdom, I'll be one with the Bread, the true Bread, Jesus Christ.

If you have a theology that emphasizes Jesus as taking care of humanity's material needs, that's all right, but I want you to graduate today and accept Jesus the Lord and Savior, Jesus who reigns over humanity, Jesus, the great King of kings and Lord of lords, Jesus, the True Bread, Jesus who offered up His body for us, His blood for us, so that we might be redeemed and liberated to life from death. Jesus! Jesus! Will you come with me and follow Him? Will you follow Him this year? Will you pick up your cross, deny yourself, and follow Him? Jesus. Will you be like the little boy who gave all that he had? He understood that little is big when you put it in the Master's hand. Jesus, Jesus, Jesus.

It doesn't take a Ph.D. It doesn't take a big bankroll. It doesn't take posturing giants in the community. What it takes is ordinary people, like you and me, to do our parts. We'll hold up the name of Jesus.

J. Alfred Smith, Jr.

8
Giving Big Brother a Loan

Luke 16:27-28

I like that part of "Amazing Grace" that goes "Thro' many dangers, toils, and snares, I have already come," t'was grace, grace. Do you know how you got over? Grace, "and grace will," God bless you.

This text is most simple. "Foxes have holes, and the birds of the air have nests; but the Son of man has nowhere to lay his head" (Matt. 8:20; Luke 9:58, RSV). I can remember how it was when my wife and I had five children living with us under the same roof. There were some exciting, challenging times. There were times when I didn't know whether I was going to be able to pay all of the bills and then buy growing boys the shoes they needed.

One of the sons, and I will not give you his name lest you would recognize him, had a way of winning the heart of his mother whenever there was a contest between him and me. Mother and this lad wanted to wear shoes that were in style. I knew that the shoes in style wouldn't last long, so I decided to purchase him some big old brogans. Mother fussed at me because I did that, and one day he decided to settle it. We were traveling from a small church I served in Columbia, Missouri, to visit my mother. When we were about a mile from Mama's house this lad reported, "I lost my shoes."

I asked, "Son, what did you do with them?"

He replied, "I threw them out the window." I wanted to stop the car to retrieve his shoes.

He confessed, "Well, Dad, I threw them out way back yonder."

That's how it is in being a parent. If you can survive being a parent, having all those kids in your house at the same time, eating up your piece of the dessert, stealing your ties, wearing your socks, and putting them back in the drawer with a hole in them, then you can testify it was grace that brought you thus far! As I reflect on how it was having all of those children under the same roof at the same time, I'm amazed at the fact that we had five, and they were all stair steps. But the youngest one would always have money. If his cash flow was low he wasn't worried, because his sister owed him and that brother owed him, and somehow he was going to collect it all. He always had money, and it amazed me when I saw him give big sister and big brother a loan.

The little brother gave the big brother a loan, and that's the topic of this sermon. Isn't Jesus our Big Brother? The Bible, in the Book of Colossians, tells us that "He is . . . the first-born of all creation" (1:15, RSV). That means He's Big Brother. The Gospel of John states, "In the beginning was the Word, and the Word was with God, and the Word was God. All things were made by him; and without him was not anything made that was made" (1:1,3). Since Jesus did all of that He's our Big Brother, but there is a paradox about the personality of Jesus, the priceless Prince of Peace. That paradox is the fact that He who made everything on earth did not have anything. He was in the beginning before there was a then or there or a when or where. He who stepped out on the scaffold of nothing and called creative worlds into existence in His humanity did not have anything. "Foxes have holes, and the birds of the air have nests; but the Son of man has nowhere to lay his head." In other words, we have a Christ that has need! I want you to pray with me. I want to present my thesis with your prayerful help. The Christ who multiplied fish and loaves, the Christ who turned water into wine, the Christ who had command over nations, the Christ who said "all power in heaven and earth is given unto me," is the same Jesus who said the "Foxes have holes; and the birds of the air have nests; but the Son of man has nowhere to lay his head."

Oh, what a paradox. This Christ who is our Elder Brother, this Christ who is Alpha and Omega, wants something from us. Yet, most of us when we come to our church and to other churches don't think about what Christ wants from us. We think about what we want from Him. I hear it in many ways. Every minister of the gospel who has been preaching any time, whether that minister is a pastor or evangelist, has heard folks remark, "I didn't get anything out of the service today." You came with your hands out, wanting to know "What's in it for me?" But Jesus is here with His hands out, wanting to know what you are going to give Him.

First of all:

Jesus Was a Borrowing Jesus

He had to borrow a manger for a cradle. He had no bed in the Mercy Hospital of Bethelem or in the General Hospital of Bethelem where poor babies, whose parents didn't have Medicare, were born. His folks were poorer than poorer. He was born in a stable. His parents had to borrow a manger, a food trough where animals came to eat, to lay Him in. But I'm so glad that Jesus identifies with those at the bottom.

If you read your paper they keep writing about the separation developing between middle-class blacks and underclass blacks. Why do they continue dwelling on that point? While the economy is bad the media is going to divert our minds from the issue that the Pentagon spent enough on one submarine to substantially upgrade education. Detractors want us to fight one another. I may not be white, but I'm not an underclassed black, but I'm so glad that Jesus had to borrow a manger for a cradle in because He came and touched life at its lowest point, letting us know it's not where we were born but where we are going that counts! Thank You, Jesus.

Single parents, let Jesus have your baby's manger. You ought to sing, "Jesus loves me! this I know." Sing to that baby. Sing to that baby, single parent. We don't have enough strong male images. We have some, but I wish we had more, but Jesus was a real man. If you can cause that child to hear the name of Jesus, there in that manger, you are making spiritual progress.

I'm thankful that where you were born and how you were born doesn't count. Because if that were so, George Washington had every right to be President because he was born wealthy and Abraham Lincoln, who was born in a log cabin, would have had no right to be President. It that were so, John Johnson, who gave a million dollars—not to the Negro College Fund (you ought to hear me now, not to one of the great black churches of America, like Hartford where Dr. Adams is pastor, or in Chicago where Dr. Wright is pastor, but he gave a million to Dr. Schuller's Crystal Cathedral)—would have had no right. He has every right. Our friend, George Washington Carver, who was born a slave, wouldn't have had a right to be a renowned scientist except God took up His abode down here in a manger. When you rise upon your feet you can look back over your humble beginnings and say, "Thro' many dangers, toils, and snares, I have already come." I didn't make it on my politics, I didn't make it on my popularity— but by grace.

A borrowing Christ not only borrowed a manger in which to be born, but one day He borrowed a boat. In the Gospel of Mark we read where Jesus was teaching on the seashore and the crowd grew so big He had to borrow a boat to use for His pulpit. That means Jesus does not have a localized pulpit.

What if God merely relegated us to the pulpit in the church building? Then only churchgoing folks would hear the gospel, but the pulpit ought to be in the building, and it also ought to be out there where Jesus' pulpit was. Jesus preached from a porch of the temple, Jesus preached by a well to the woman of Samaria. Jesus preached from a fishing boat. It was made to deal with economics, to fish in the sea of Galilee. Yet, Jesus wanted to use a fishing boat that was used in catching fish to "fish" after the souls of men.

Yes, your job ought to be a pulpit. You ought to share Jesus with your fellow workers. If you can't call the name of Jesus, they should be able to look at you and see that there's something different about you, that you've been touched from on high. Jesus wants to borrow a pulpit today, borrow your home, or borrow your sidewalk, borrow your neighborhood, borrow your job to tell men and women, "I am the way, the truth, and the life. No man cometh to the Father but by me" (John 14:6). A borrowed pulpit.

Not only did He borrow a pulpit, but one day He borrowed a little boy's lunch. Do you remember that? Jesus used five loaves of bread, two small fish, and multiplied that borrowed lunch to feed a hungry multitude. I used not to take time to dig deep when I studied the Word of God. I tried to cover as many pages as I could to see if I could learn as much as I could. But I learned that when you really read the Word of God, you don't rush over it. You take your time and work with every word. So I simply kept wrestling with that word *barley, barley* loaves. Why barley loaves? Well, every word in the Bible means something. *Barley* meant the poor man's food. Rich men didn't eat barley loaves.

It's like when I was a boy in Kansas City. I lived with my uncle and aunt for awhile. You ought to go back and think about from whence you've come. Never rise so high that you forget your roots. In my humble abode with my uncle, we had to take his lunch to the railroad track. He was a stevedore, a laborer, yes he was, on the Missouri Pacific Railroad. Poor folks in those days didn't have much. All they had was sardines and crackers. And sometimes, crackers and cheese. That's all that a hardworking man had. That little boy's lunch was like soda crackers. Where I came from they called them soda crackers.

Jesus took what that little boy had. Yes, He did, and fed a hungry multitude. I like that about Jesus, He wants to borrow. The reason He had the little boy's lunch is because the little boy gave himself first. You can't give your all to Jesus unless you give yourself first. He first gave himself to Jesus. Yes, in East Oakland, social workers have written little boys off. Educators have written little black boys off. Society has written them off. You act like you don't know what I'm talking about. They're building jails for little black boys, bigger jails, not bigger schools. They'd rather pay $15,000 to $30,000 a year to keep a black boy in jail than to send him to Stanford.

But I know Somebody. What's His name? Jesus, the Lamb of God. Jesus—Mary's baby. Jesus, the Lily of the Valley. Jesus, the Bright and Morning Star. He wants your boy. He wants your girl. And whatever talent that child has, He'll multiply it. Yes, Oh Lord. I see Jesus borrowing a donkey. He borrowed a donkey and rode it to Jerusalem. And as he rode into the city on a donkey, they yelled, "Hosanna, Blessed is he that cometh in the name of the Lord" (Mark 11:9). I don't know whether you're riding in a Cadillac or a Volkswagen. I don't know whether you are riding in a BMW or a Ford, but you ought to bring somebody to church. Jesus wants to borrow your transportation. Let Him use your transportation. Some senior citizen, somebody without a car, some blind person, some child needs a ride to church to hear some saints say, "I can tell the world about this, tell the nation I'm blessed." Tell them that the Comforter has come, and that He brought joy, joy, joy to our souls.

I thank You, Lord, You brought me a mighty long way. Well, Jesus borrowed a grave. He died on a Friday, died on a cross, died between two thieves, died with a crown of thorns on His head, died with nails in His feet. He died, begged for forgiveness for his executioners, and during His seven words He cried out, "Father, into thy hands I commend my spirit" (Luke 24:46). They took Him down from the cross, and Joseph of Arimathea, a wealthy man, took His body and put it for three days in the tomb.

Jesus said, "I won't need it very long. Joseph. I'm going to give it back to you, Joseph. I want to stay there Friday night and Saturday night." But early Sunday morning He rose up. Yes, He did. All power was in His hands. Yes, when I come to die, I'm not worried whether or not I'll have a big funeral. I'm not worried whether or not they'll have a crowd. I'm not worried about the resolutions. I'm not worried about whether my preacher friends will come to my funeral. But what I want is for Jesus to go into my tomb, get there with me, and I want Him to say, "Smith, we're just going to borrow this spot at Rolling Hills for a little while. Because 'I am the resurrection, and the life: he that believeth in me, though he were dead, yet shall he live.' "

I'm so glad that we serve a borrowing Jesus, for one day He borrowed your sins, and he borrowed my sins on a cross. "All we like sheep have gone astray, we have turned every one to his own way; and the Lord hath laid on him the iniquity of us all" (Isa. 53:6). Thank You, Jesus! Thank You, Jesus! You borrowed my sins and gave me a new name in glory. You borrowed my sins and gave me a sweet gospel to preach. You borrowed my sins and gave me the Holy Spirit. Thank You, Lord! You've brought me a mighty long way. When I was sick, You healed me, and when I was dying You raised me. Thank You, Jesus, thank You!

God bless you. I see a lady walking down the aisle. Last time I saw her, in the hospital, I didn't know whether she'd live or climb off of her bed, but I want you to know that the Lord has brought Sister Phillips a mighty long way. I want to speak with sweetness this morning. I don't want to speak critically or bitterly, but some of us who have been steeped in the philosophy of rationalism have come to the point where we are ashamed of expressing even a sanctified emotion. What bothers me is that those same pseudo-intellectuals will go to party and pay top dollar. Many haven't been to church all year, but they will go to a party and drink expensive Scotch whisky.

May our Big Brother call us away from our hollowness, our self-centeredness, and pretense. May we determine to give Him our all.

JAS, Sr.

9
One Hundred Percent Arrangement

2 Corinthians 8:1-5

Our text is from the *Good News Bible,* the Bible in Today's English Version, 2 Corinthians 8:1-5.

> Our brothers, we want you to know what God's grace has accomplished in the churches in Macedonia. They have been severely tested by the troubles they went through; but their joy was so great that they were extremely generous in their giving, even though they are very poor. I can assure you that they gave as much as they could, and even more than they could. Of their own free will they begged us and pleaded for the privilege of having a part in helping God's people in Judea. It was more than we could have hoped for! First they gave themselves to the Lord; and then, by God's will they gave themselves to us as well.

Not what we expected, but more. In fact, much more than we could hope for. Those churches were far more generous than what seemed reasonable. These churches in Macedonia were young in age and small in membership. Affliction and persecution were their daily companions. Poverty had touched their lives deeply. They knew what it was to be without, what it was to run short of having enough to make it because poverty had permeated their lives to the core. Very few of their membership belonged to the business and professional class. In fact, biblical historians tell us that those who did have possessions had lost many of them as the result of an earthquake in Macedonia. And those who did not lose their possessions through the earthquake had been stripped of them by the Romans, since the people of Macedonia were occupied by oppressive colonial forces. Few of them had "bragging rights." Yet these simple, Christ-loving, God-fearing, compassionate-feeling people were moved with merciful generosity when they learned that the apostle Paul was raising an offering for the famine-stricken churches of Jerusalem.

I've never been able to understand it. It's a mystery to me how those who often are the most blessed are the most selfish, whereas those who struggle seem to be willing to share their crust of bread with another beggar who's begging. This is the way it was in 2 Corinthians 8:1-5. Listen to Paul tell us about the churches in Macedonia. In verses 1 and 2, Paul explains, "We want you to know what God's grace has accomplished in the churches of Macedonia. They have been severely tested by the troubles they went through; but their joy was so great that they were extremely generous in their giving, even though they are very poor" (GNB).

What a Contrast

What a paradox, what a contrast, what an extreme! They were extremely poor because of their afflictions, because of their troubles. But, on the other hand, they were most joyful in the generosity of their giving. In other words, very joyful in the generosity of their giving because they gave without complaining. That ought to be a message to us today, for the Bible says, "Serve the Lord with gladness" (Ps. 100:2). Serve the Lord, not with complaining, not with criticism, but "Serve the Lord with gladness." They had been severely tested by trouble. Do you hear me? They had been knocked down on their backs, yet they had the joyous generosity of saying "Thank You, Jesus" by giving to somebody who was worse off than they.

An old expression goes, "And I cried because I had no shoes until I met a man who had no feet." There's always somebody worse off than you. You may be feeling sorry for yourself, but there is somebody whose every breath is predicated on a machine doing the work of the human lungs. You ought to say "thank You, Jesus."

The Macedonian church taught us three stern realities: (1) they were poor; (2) they were severely tested by troubles, and (3) their joy was great. Because their joy was great they wanted to help the famine-stricken brothers and sisters in Jerusalem. Paul stated in verses 3 and 4, "I can assure you that they gave as much as they could, and even more than they could. Of their own free will they begged us and pleaded for the privilege for having a part in helping God's people in Judea" (GNB). When I reflect on those words of sacred Scripture, I'm reminded of the fact that God does not expect you, and God does not expect me, to do it all. All He wants us to do is to have a part. He expects us, and He desires of us, to have a share. He expects us to make our contributions. And verses 3 and 4 tell us that they begged Paul to let them have a part in this missionary endeavor.

The Christians of Macedonia were saying: "Yes, we're very poor. Yes, we're severely tested by trouble but, in spite of it all, God has been good to us. We want to have a share in helping the brothers and sisters in Judea." Reason and logic are both cold and dispassionate. Reason and logic are not emotional. Reason and logic are very practical. So those of you with an argumentative nature, that grows out of the context of reason and logic, are saying as you hear this message. "How can very poor, severely troubled Christians be happy, and at the same time unselfish?"

What a Secret

What was their secret? What was the motivation for their behavior? How can I believe there were people who actually behaved as reported in 2 Corinthians 8? Verse 1 gives us a partial answer. Paul explains it this way. He says, "We want you to know what God's grace has accomplished in the churches of Macedonia." In other words, generosity in people is the work of God's grace. By nature you and I are selfish. By nature we come here with our hands closed. By nature little children have closed fists. Spiritually, many of us are still little children.

My friend, who is now in heaven, Dr. Jackson of Tulsa, Oklahoma, told of a time when he was shaking hands with his parishioners as they were leaving the church. A little boy came by with his mother. He wanted to give that little boy a dollar, but the little boy wouldn't open up his hands. Dr. Jackson explained that the mother said, "Well, the reason why he's not opening his hand is that he has a quarter in it. He felt that if he shook your hand, he would lose his quarter." The Bible says that God loves a cheerful giver so much that the Word—not Pastor J. Alfred Smith—said, "He which soweth sparingly, shall reap also sparingly" (2 Cor. 9:6).

The Word lets us know that by nature, human beings are self-centered, narrow-minded, and greedy. Grace enables us, God's grace and not ours, to say when it comes to giving generously, "I once was lost, on this issue of giving, but now I've found that God's Word is true. Not because the preacher said so, but I have been touched by the grace of God." God's grace redeems. God's grace saves. God's grace converts. God's grace helps Christians to behave as the Christians did in Macedonia. Arm twisting, sales promotions, Sunday morning pep talks, and pulpit pleadings will not produce cheerful giving that pleases God. If the Word of God does not do it, if God's grace doesn't take the Word and convince, nurture, and change us, public relations won't do it.

What a Grace

The grace of God must touch you. The grace of God must touch me. The grace of God must touch immature persons of little faith and convert us into understanding that God has called us to be servants. Many of us want positions, but it's not the position that makes the person. It's the sacrifice that the person contributes in the position. If God's grace was at work in the churches of Macedonia, and if God's grace was a partial answer for the motivation of the Macedonian Christians, what is the other answer for their generosity? I call it, as I meditate upon the Scriptures, the "100 Percent Arrangement." For verse 5 tells us, "First," and will you repeat after me? "First they gave themselves to the Lord" (GNB). We have so many in Allen Temple and in other churches—

and I don't want to pick on any other church, so I'll just say *us*—who are here but do not give ourselves to the Lord. Do you understand? We're here. Good music brought us here. Good singing brought us here. A good organist brought us here. The reputation of the church brought us here. A friend brought us here. But I want to know first, have we met the Lord?

I'm going to take my time and teach the simple Word of God. "First, they gave themselves to the Lord. And then, by God's will they gave themselves to us as well" (GNB). What is this talk about first giving themselves to God? "Preacher, how do we accomplish first giving ourselves to God?" Well, church members, and especially church officers, must acknowledge the reality of God. It's hard for us to acknowledge the reality of a God we can't see. I can see this handkerchief. I can see this Bible. I can see you looking at me, and I can see those stained-glass windows, but I can't see God. And because we come here Sunday after Sunday with only the physical eyes, we know what somebody else had on. We saw where somebody was sitting, we saw somebody usher, we saw somebody sing, but did we see God? Were we made aware of the reality of God? Unless you are aware of the reality of God, it's a waste of time to attend church.

People join churches for many reasons but not enough of them experience the reality of God. Ask yourself, if you are aware of the reality of God at work in your own life. And how aware are you of God's reality in your own heart? What is God doing to expand your thinking? What is God doing to stretch your patience and your toleration? What is God doing to make you more compassionate and more merciful? What about the reality of God in your life? If you are aware of the reality of God in your heart, can you then move from reality to respect for God? When we respect God we believe His Word, and we try to obey His Word. When you respect God you try to please Him. Second Corinthians 9:7 says, "For God loves the one who gives gladly" (GNB). Now there is both the reality of God and the Christian respect for God, but there is also the right relationship with God.

In Psalm 51:10 we're taught to pray, "Create in me a clean heart, O God, and renew a right spirit within me." A right spirit has healing in it. A right spirit is a loving spirit. A right spirit is a merciful spirit. A right spirit does not rejoice when a sister or brother has a bad time, or when a brother or sister makes a mistake. That's the Word of God, not J. Alfred Smith. You may have a problem with me, but that's not important. I can't save you, but do you have a problem with what God said? God said "Blessed are the merciful: for they shall obtain mercy" (Matt. 5:7). You can't give any mercy. You may be traveling high and mighty, but your day is going to come.

"Create a pure heart in me, O God, and put a new and loyal spirit in me" (GNB). We can't be loyal to one another because we haven't been loyal to God. I don't know how to make it plain. Our awareness of God's reality, our respect for God, our right relationship with God will teach us first to give ourselves to the Lord. Give yourself to Jesus. You don't have much time. I said give yourself. We give ourselves to an office in the church. We give ourselves to a position in the church. We give ourselves to the membership in the church, but we are not going to be judged by any of that. Give yourself to God. Surrender your will to Him. Sacrifice your all to Him. Share your gift for God's purpose and God's program.

What an Arrangement

What is your arrangement with God, brothers and sisters? I repeat: what is your arrangement with God? How much do you love God? If you could get an insurance policy to insure your love to God, would you pay for full coverage, or would you pay for 50 percent coverage? Think about it today. What is your love cash flow in obedience to God? I want to know what your arrangement is to God. What is your love cash flow in obedience to God? What is your love cash flow in evangelism? What are your love contributions to God in terms of your time, in terms of your talents, and in terms of your tithes? If God blessed you in terms of how you invested your time, talents, and tithes, would He have awakened you this morning? Would He have clothed you in your right mind? Would He have started you on your way? If God would have forgiven you, on the basis of whether you have forgiven your brother and sister in church, would you attend church at all?

Many people in our churches claim that the preacher should preach less and teach more. I've heard that we need more teaching. The pulpit responds then by asking are you teachable? Have you a barrier to accepting the sacred Word of Scripture? Do you really believe that the Scripture is God's Word? Do you really believe that the Bible is the authority for our faith and practice? Do you have a disciplined approach to the study of God's Word? Can you say, "Thy word is a lamp unto my feet, and a light unto my path"? (Ps. 119:105). Well, I must teach a little bit.

"Pastor, preachers should preach less and teach more." If that is true, why do we have such a crowd in the breezeway between the sanctuary and the Sunday School classroom? The question is, are you teachable? What is your spirit? You have to be openminded in order to learn. You have to be openhearted if you want to grow. How is your arrangement with God? Who owns the most of you, God or Satan? How much of your conscience does God own, and how much of your conversation does Satan own? How much of your cash flow does God own. Who do you make your love contributions to, God or Satan? Is your compassion controlled by the grace of God? How is your arrangement with God? And when the Holy Spirit gives you new life in Christ, does your theme song become "I Surrender All"?

What a Warfare

We are in a war, and some of us are in the Lord's army, and some of us are in Satan's army. Some of us are in the Lord's army in disguise as double agents of Satan, but the Lord's army is going to win the war. The Lord's army is going to march victoriously into the new Jerusalem just like John. The Lord's army is going to march in Jerusalem and say, "All hail the power of Jesus' name." If I were fighting in Satan's army, if I were a double agent in the church, but my real allegiance were to Satan, I'd surrender. I'd surrender while I still had time. Yes, if I were on the wrong side, if I were a prisoner of dope, you ought to hear me. If I were a prisoner of drugs, a prisoner of alcohol, a prisoner of selfishness, a prisoner of gossip, a prisoner of meanness, a prisoner of orneriness, a prisoner of hypocrisy, I'd surrender right now. I'd say:

> All to Jesus I surrender,
> All to Him I freely give;
> I will ever love and trust Him,
> In His presence daily live.
> I surrender all,
> I surrender all;
> All to Thee, my blessed Savior,
> I surrender all.

(Words by *J. W. Van DeVenter*)

You've been my bread. You've been my water in dry places. You've fought my battles. You've rocked me in the arms of mercy.

Yes, I surrender all. Yes. I'm so glad I don't have to fight my battles. I surrender. I put it in the Lord's hands. If you have a child that you can't do anything with, surrender him or her. Give that child to Jesus. Admiral Toney came to see me, and we went to lunch the other day. He said, "Pastor Smith, I'm concerned if the Navy leaves Oakland, we're going to lose 44,000 jobs." Well, I can't do anything about all of these problems. I'm not the fix-it man but I know the real fix-it Man. I'm going to turn it loose and give it to Jesus. I'm going to surrender it to Jesus. I'm going to lean on Jesus.

I surrendered my life to Christ a long time ago. Somebody may want to do that right now. I'm concerned about your personal arrangement with God. I'm not the fix-it man. It's not my job to fix everything that's broken. But I just put it in the hand of God and let Him straighten it out.

Do you know Him for yourself? What's your arrangement? You might have a good arrangement for time, but do you have a good arrangement for eternity?

JAS, Sr.

10
What to Give the Christ

Matthew 21:1-10

This same story with different variations is found in the other Gospels (Mark 11:1-11; Luke 19:28-40; and John 12:12-19). The other Gospels present the same story, but each adds something which the others do not relate. I have chosen to speak from Matthew's account.

About two weeks ago, a young lad came to the secretary's desk and asked to see me. She told him I was very busy, and he needed an appointment (and I was *very* busy). But he was a member of our church, and I felt I should forget about my schedule and disappoint the people I was to see. The first thing he said to me was, "Pastor Smith, you know I haven't been coming to church."

I said, "I know that, and I wonder what's wrong."

He said, "Pastor Smith, I need help, and I've been too ashamed to come to church. I have a drug problem."

I told him that the church is a hospital for sinners, and not a museum for saints. I took him by the hand, like I would take my children, even though he was taller than me and led him into the Allen Temple Haight-Ashbury Recovery Center, located at 1301 86th Avenue.

That young man is being treated there in confidence. I'm not going to tell his name, and nobody else is going to tell his name. Isn't that wonderful? That's what the church is supposed to do, not only give you a ticket for heaven but to help you to have life and have it more abundantly here on earth (see John 10:10). That's what church is all about. You can't take that record away from a true church. You can say whatever you want to say of a critical nature, but you just can't say that a true church doesn't have a grief ministry. You just can't say that we don't have a ministry for people getting out of jail and people in jail. You just can't say we don't have a recovery center. You just can't say that we don't have a youth program. You just can't say that we don't have a staff. If you call this church tomorrow somebody's going to answer the telephone. Isn't that a fact? And shouldn't we thank God?

Thanks to our trustee chairlady, Verdell Brooks, who is helping us with the board of trustees to expand our center. Our trustee chairlady was an original member of our prison ministry team. Last night she was honored by the National Association of Black Public Administrators as being the Outstanding Educator of the Year. Yet she will still work in the kitchen. She's not a big shot. She is a servant. Let's encourage each other.

Will you repeat after me, "What can we give to Christ who has everything?" The Christ I serve has everything. The Christ I serve is the Son of God who left heaven and gave His life as a ransom for your salvation and mine. There are other Christs, you know. There is the Unitarian Christ. The Unitarian Church sees Jesus merely as another man. He was human but no more God than Guatama Buddha. He was human and no more God than Muhammad the prophet, who claimed God was named Allah. They say that Jesus "became" the Son of God, and they put emphasis on the word *became*. The ministers in training under me, who have studied with Dr. George Cummings at the American Baptist Seminary of the West, have learned that this view of Christ is called adoptionist Christianity, that Jesus was born as human as you are but no more God than you and me. But somehow because this Christ opened Himself up to God at His baptism, He was adopted as the Son of God, and you and I both have the same ability to become like this Christ. In other words, you and I can become little Christs.

I'm worried about that definition of Jesus, I am concerned about the Jehovah's Witnesses's definition of Jesus. The Jehovah's Witnesses claim that Jesus was the firstborn of creation, and therefore they subtract from Him the power of His deity. And that concept of Jesus is what I would call a reductionism of Christ. It reduces Christ to less than what John said. He said "In the beginning was the Word, and the Word was with God, and the Word was God. All things were made by him; and without him was not anything made that was made. And the word was made flesh and dwelt among us" (John 1:1,3,14). Now, if you believe that, then you believe in a Christ who has everything. The Christ who has everything is the same Christ that multiplied the fish and loaves. The Christ who has everything is the same Christ that took mud and did what the American Medical Association would call unsanitary. He spit in that mud and made a medicinal salve and put it on a man's eyes and told him to go and wash. Then the blind man was able to see. This is a Christ who has everything. Christ, who has everything, was sleeping in a boat one day, and a storm came up. A disciple said, "We'd better wake up Jesus because He has everything." He has power over nature, and Jesus rebuked the wind and the waves. And the disciples asked, "What manner of man is this, that even the winds and the sea obey him!" (Matt. 8:27). The Christ who has everything.

One day this Christ was en route from Jericho to Jerusalem. It was to be His final journey. It was "the beginning of the end," for four days later He was going to sit down at the table with the twelve. After supper He was going to be arrested. On Friday they were going to kill Him. From that cross He uttered seven words. Before He reached the city of Jerusalem, He stood on the Mount of Olives, and looked down toward the city, and instructed two disciples, "I want you to run ahead now and go into a village, the other village." One was called Bethphage, and the other, Bethany. I've been to Bethany. That's the village He told them to enter, Bethany the city where Lazarus was buried. Jesus had commanded, "Get up, Lazarus, I'm the Christ who has everything. I even have power over death." And He said, "In that village you're going to see two animals, a female donkey and beside her is her little colt. I want you to untie them."

"And he said now if they say anything to you, I want you to tell him that the Lord has needs" (Matt: 21:2-3, Author). Isn't that a mystery? The Christ who has everything had a need. The Lord has needs. He has everything, yet He had a need. What do you buy a person who has everything? When I'm shopping I know what to get my children because they don't have everything. When I'm shopping I know what to get my grandchildren because I looked at them and saw this one needed shoes and another needed a shirt or another needed a necktie, and I saw that one had just worn out shoes that their daddy and mama had bought them two weeks before! I said, "I know what they need, but what do you get somebody that's doing well?" I don't know what to buy some of our well-to-do church members, because you have everything. Almost everything. But Jesus has everything, doesn't He? He said He had all power—all power in heaven and earth is in His hand. What do you give a Christ who has everything? Matthew 21:6 tells us, "So the disciples went and did what Jesus had told them to do: they brought the donkey and the colt, and threw their cloaks over them, and Jesus got on" (GNB).

The first truth the disciples are teaching us is that if we are disciples, we must do what Jesus tells us to do. How hard is that? That's hard. Sometimes pride gets in the way. Sometimes arrogance is an obstacle. Sometimes sensitivity stands in the way or sometimes ego is a barrier. Sometimes you say and I say, "No, Lord, not Your will, but my will." But, if you don't know what to give the Christ who has everything, first of all you can give Him obedience.

The disciples did what Jesus told them to do. There are some folks at our church that you do not speak to, and you ought to speak to them. There are some folks in your family, maybe your mama, your daddy, your uncle, your brother, your cousin, your sister, or your nephew who you aren't speaking to. When I was in Rustin, Louisiana, conducting a citywide revival, I invited married couples to come to the altar for prayer. Some came holding hands; the others came six feet behind each other! When I told them to hold hands at the altar, some never held hands. Jesus said, "A new commandment I give unto you" (John 13:34). A new commandment that you do what? *Love one another*. "Love your enemies, do good to them that hate you, and pray for them which despitefully use you" (Matt. 5:44). What are we going to do? Are we going to do what the Master said to do? We ought to do what He has asked us to do, namely, to love one another.

The disciples did what Jesus told them to do. They brought the donkey and the colt. But before they could bring that donkey and that colt, they had to untie the colt and the donkey. There are some folks that are tied up in Oakland this morning. They need to be untied from bad habits. Untie them from drugs. Untie them from alcohol. Untie them from depression. If you're depressed you're a slave. How can you be tied down to depression and defeat when you serve a Christ who has everything? Lord, liberate your people.

The disciples knew what to do, but the man that owned the donkey and the colt also knew what to do. He gave up his personal possessions. He gave them to Jesus. Yes, when we give our tithes and our offerings, we are not giving them to Pastor J. Alfred Smith, to the Allen Temple Trustee Board, or even to Allen Temple Church. Once tithes and offerings have been dedicated with prayer, they are a gift to the Lord. See the owner of the donkey and colt. I can hear him say, "Well, the Master can have this donkey. That donkey is getting old but leave me my colt." The colt had never been ridden. That's what the Bible indicated. Jesus was the first one to ride the colt. When I think about the reason why some of us have not been broken, it's because Jesus hasn't ridden us. The reason why some of us are cold, callous, mean, and selfish is that we haven't been broken in by Jesus. We'd better let Jesus change our lives. Old folks call it conversion. They used to say: "I looked at my hands, they looked new, I looked at my feet, and they did, too." Jesus had transformed their lives.

What was the man's name? The story is told in all four Gospels. Mark doesn't tell us his name. Matthew doesn't tell us his name.

WHAT TO GIVE THE CHRIST

Luke doesn't tell his name. John doesn't tell us his name. But he didn't say, "I'll let you have my donkey and my colt if you put my name in the record, if you would give me a plaque, if you would pin a boutonniere on me, if you would bring me in front of the church and let the church know that I did it." We don't even know the man's name. But Jesus knows. Sometimes when you do good and sometimes when you give money, nobody ought to know about it because if they do, then your critics can criticize your motive for giving. "Oh, he did that." "She gave just to show off." "He gave that." "He gave for this reason or that reason." Or if you do it, and don't get criticized, then maybe somebody will just try to match you. But whatever you do for Christ, it ought to be in His name and it ought to be in His Spirit and for His glory. Jesus said that if you give secretly God will reward you openly.

The anonymous gift and the anonymous giver—or the donkey and the colt the giver gave up. He gave them to Jesus. When I gave my life to Jesus I did it in the privacy of a moment. There was nobody but the Lord and me. When the Lord called me to preach, it was a private transaction. I had to make it known publicly. That means you and I ought to have private times with the Lord. When it comes time for you to die, it won't be anybody but God and you. It won't be the doctor. It won't be mother. It won't be father. It won't be the pastor. It won't be friends, but it will be you and the Lord. But if God is on speaking terms with you, and if you are on speaking terms with Him, you can say, "Yea, though I walk through the valley of the shadow of death, I will fear no evil: for thou art with me" (Ps. 23:4).

What do you give to the Christ who has everything? The Bible said that there were three crowds. There was the crowd that came out from Jerusalem to meet Jesus as He rode that little colt. There was the crowd with Jesus coming up from Jericho and Bethany. And there were the disciples. One of the faults of my preaching this text in previous years, yes, for nineteen years is that I have handled it inadequately. I didn't preach it the wrong way; I just talked about the Palm Sunday crowd that lifted Jesus up and then yelled "Crucify Him" on Good Friday. They exalted him on Palm Sunday and then on Good Friday they said "Crucify him." I merely preached that point of view.

But thank you, Jesus, thank you for the rain yesterday. Old J. Alfred Smith didn't have anything to do but enter his study, close the door, and have a little talk with Jesus. And the Lord said, "Close up those commentaries, I'm your commentary." He said, "I want to show you something that you haven't seen before. You have been giving too much attention to the negative. You have just been talking about the folks that are against Me. You have just been preaching about the Palm Sunday crowd that was fickle, the crowd that just said 'glory.' But they didn't mean it. You've just been preaching about the two-faced crowd that would say 'Hosanna' on Palm Sunday and say 'Crucify Him' on Good Friday. But that's a negative gospel. You've been giving the negative folks too much press."

Sometimes in the church we give the negative people too much press. If somebody is sleeping next to you, elbow them because they need to hear this. There are a lot of good people in the church. Yes, they don't gossip. They come here to meet the Lord. There are a lot of good folks in the church who have been born again. We had better stop giving the negative crowd so much exposure and realize that in that crowd there were some folks who loved the Lord. They gave Him the palm branches, and the palms were symbolic of victory. I want to know, do you have a palm branch this morning?

In Kansas City, Missouri, at the Pilgrim Rest Baptist Church, where I found the Lord, Palm Sunday was almost as exciting as Easter—because they would pin on us little children palm branches and when we went into the church they had palm branches. The palm branches were a victory sign. I don't have time to argue it, but in the apocryphal Book of 1 Maccabees, when Judas Maccabeus had won the battle against the Romans, they waved palm branches (see 1 Macc. 10:7). Yes. Jesus was riding on a donkey. They were waving, and He was the King. You're going to crucify Him on Friday, but He's the King. Death is going to grab Him Friday, but

He's the King. He's the King that has everything. Just tear this body down, tear down this temple. In three days it's going to rise again. You ought to be waving a palm branch. Yes, if you are a victorious Christian, if you've got Christ in your life, you ought to wave a palm branch. I don't care how many burdens you have in your life, you ought to wave a palm branch. I don't care how much trouble there is in your life, you ought to wave a palm branch. I serve a victorious Savior. I serve a God who has power. I serve a God who makes a way out of no way. All power is in his hands. "He's got the whole world in His hands. He's got the little [bitty] baby in His hands." Ride on, ride on King Jesus, ride on conquering King.

JAS, Sr.

11
Treasure or Trash

John 1:10-11

"He came unto his own, and his own received him not. But as many as received him, to them gave he power to become the sons of God" (John 1:11-12).

"What do you want?

My wife and I have been traveling all the way from Galilee to Bethlehem."

"You mean that you and this pregnant woman have come all the way from Galilee to Judea? Why are you here?"

"As you know, a decree has come from Caesar Augustus that all the world should be taxed. And it was necessary for us to leave our humble village Nazareth in northern Galilee to come down into the heart of Judea here to register. We must pay our taxes, you know."

"Why are you knocking on my door at this hour of the night? Why are you disturbing me and my wife?"

"Well, Sir, as you have already noticed, my wife is pregnant and it's cold outside, and we don't have any place to stay."

"Who was that?"

"Some trash from Galilee, some freeloaders wanting to spend the night with us."

On and on they went, knocking on doors, asking for a place to stay. But no one had room in their hearts, nor in their homes for them, because, you see, they were considered trash. Maybe they went to the synagogues, and perhaps they were closed during the week. For the rabbis would have services on the Sabbath, collect their money, and then go home. The members would enjoy the singing of the choirs and say, "Let's wait again until next Sabbath, and if the trash would be good and serve God like we do, He would bless them. They're in this condition because they haven't served the Lord."

So finally, because God had decreed, a little innkeeper, who had no more room in his inn, said, "You homeless woman, you homeless man, you unborn baby, you can spend the night here. Since welfare wouldn't help you, you can spend the night here." "And she brought forth her firstborn son, and wrapped him in swaddling clothes [or rags], and laid him in a manger" (Luke 2:7).

The baby was treated like trash, but Mary was not trash. She was treasure. Didn't the angel Gabriel say to her, "Blessed art thou among women"? (Luke 1:28). You are blessed over the president of the Zeta Sigma Phi. You're blessed over the president of the Daughters of the American Revolution. You're blessed. "Blessed art thou among women, and blessed is the fruit of thy womb" (v. 42). She was the treasure, but she was treated like trash.

Joseph was a treasure, but he was treated like trash. The angel said, "Now, Joseph I know people are talking about you—marrying a woman and you're not the father of the child. And I know they are saying you must be a fool for believing her story that she became pregnant by the Holy Spirit. Women have been getting pregnant since the day of Adam and Eve and none of them have ever said that before, Joseph. But you are a just man and believe that God is a just God. You're not trash—you are treasure." That little baby was treated like trash, but He was a treasure because the angel told Mary, "Now when you name Him you should call His name Jesus, because He shall save His people from their sins" (Author, see Matt. 1:18-21). Jesus, the sweetest name I know; Jesus the Treasure, treated like trash.

Why do we treat treasures in our midst like trash? I see him. "Hey, taxi, give me a ride, please. I'm on my way to Congress." The taxi driver looked at the old man and saw that he had a ragged suitcase in his hand and that his suit was unpressed and that his shoes were scuffed. His hat had seen the rain of many springtimes and the snow of many cold winters. Driving by the old man, the cab driver said, "Look at him, he's nothing but a tramp." But by the providence of God, that old man who, even as a baby, was treated like trash (he was born in Diamond, Missouri, as a slave but because he was a sickly baby his owner traded him, snatched him from his mother's arms, and traded him for a broken-down race-horse), and now, as an old man, still treated like trash, made his way to Congress. When he got through showing them that he had taken the peanut and made many miraculous, unheard-of discoveries, they knew they were talking to Dr. George Washington Carver, the great scientist who is represented in the stained-glass windows of our church. On the outside he looked like trash, but the measure of a man is by his mind and not his physical appearance. Why is it that we sometimes misread treasures in our midst and treat them like trash?

When this Jewish baby grew up and became a young lad at the age of twelve, he was ready for His bar mitzvah. Every Jewish boy has a bar mitzvah at age twelve; that's the time when the Jewish boy is admitted into manhood. He went to the temple, and when the bar mitzvah was over, he was expected to live by the law of Moses. When do we initiate our young men? What are our initiation rites? When do our young men learn about their Abrahams, Isaacs, and Jacobs? When do our young men learn about their Exodus from Egypt and the God who delivered us across our Red Sea? You do believe that God did that, don't you?

Well, Jesus was so fascinated that He stayed in the temple some three days. Mary and Joseph started home, and after three days' journey the Gospel of Luke describes it in this manner. Supposing Jesus was in the company, the mother and father kept traveling. But, mothers and fathers, you should never suppose anything about your children. You ought always to know where they are or what they're supposed to be doing. They found out that Jesus was not there, and they went back to the temple after checking everywhere, because that was the last place they had seen Him. The Bible tells us that they chided Him and Jesus said to them, "How is it that ye sought me? wist ye not that I must be about my Father's business?" (2:49). In other words, sometimes parents can have a treasure in their children, but they don't even know it. So it's dangerous to tell a child, "You ain't gonna be nothing. You're just like your daddy." Or for daddy to say, "I know it, that's just like your mother's side of the family."

Some young people who have been on their way up have commented to me, "I'm trying to make it in life, new heights I'm trying to gain every day. But I have some family members who tell me I have the big head, that I want to be more than what I am." When God puts a treasure in your family, you ought not treat that person like trash; you ought to encourage that treasure. If you didn't have the opportunity, you can still inspire others to reach for the stars.

Jesus was just starting His ministry after being baptized in the river Jordan. He went to His hometown in Nazareth. He stood up that day in the synagogue to read the Scriptures. He took His text from Isaiah 61:1, "The spirit of the Lord is upon me, because he hath anointed me to preach the gospel to the poor" (Luke 4:18). And what did the audience say? "Is not this the carpenter's son?" (Matt. 13:55). ("We knew him when He grew up two blocks off of E. 14th Street. We knew him when he was struggling to get through Castlemont High School. We knew him when . . .") They had treasure in their midst, but they treated the Treasure like trash.

Yes, they did. They did that to my Lord. "He came unto His own, and His own received Him not" (John 1:11). His own didn't receive Him. He was a son of Abraham. He came through fourteen generations. Isaiah promised He was going to come. Daniel predicted he was going to come. He was Daniel's stone hewed out of the mountain (see Dan. 2:34-35). He was Isaiah's "wonderful, counselor," mighty God, everlasting Father, and Prince of Peace (see Isa. 9:6). But when He came, they didn't accept Him. They had treasure, but they treated Him like trash.

Jesus who was treated like trash, treated *every* person like treasure. Didn't He do it? Didn't He elevate a woman who was caught in the very act of adultery by the leaders, the deacons, the trustees, and the preachers? I made it plain that the preachers are in there because I don't want anybody saying that the pastor's shooting at me. Don't you know that the gospel is a two-edged sword? If it cuts you it's going to come back and cut me. But you just don't want the gospel, do you? And they said, "Lord we caught this woman in the act," but they didn't bring the man (see John 8:3-4). "The law said, the law of Moses said, the law of Moses said," Genesis, Exodus, Leviticus, Numbers, Deuteronomy. Those first five books make up the books of the Law. "Why, this woman is to be stoned. What do You say about it, Jesus? If you don't stone the woman then you're not the religious man you claim to be, because if you're a religious man, then you really have to believe what the law says." Jesus thought to Himself, *Don't they know that a greater one than Moses is here? Don't they know that before Moses was I AM? Don't they know that before the morning stars sang together, or the sons of God shouted for joy, I stepped out in space and did my work so that when John wrote about Me he said that "In the beginning was the Word, and the Word was with God, and the Word was God. And the Word became flesh and dwelt among us. All things were made by him and without him was not anything made that was made"?*

But Jesus said, "I don't have time to give them a biblical lesson. I'm going to deal in the area of reality and practicality." Jesus said, in essence, "Check yourself out. You're worrying about the woman. You're worrying about the trash that's in her life. Check yourself out. The one without sin should throw the first stone" (see vv. 6-7).

They had to drop those rocks and walk away quietly. And the Bible says the oldest left first. That meant those who had been around doing devilment the longest. Jesus looked at the woman and said, "I'm not denying that you haven't had trash in your life, but I'm going to make you a treasure. Go in peace and sin no more" (see vv. 10-11). Isn't that good news? Good news, the chariot's coming. Good news, the chariot's coming. Good news, the chariot's coming, and I don't want to be left behind."

Yes, Jesus, I see you getting up in the garden of Gethsemane.

Jesus, I see you looking for something to wipe sweat from your eyes. Jesus, you've been praying. Your heart has been heavy. You knew that Calvary was in front of you, and so you called on Your Father, and I heard you say, "Father, if it be Thy will, let this bitter cup pass from me; nevertheless, not My will, not My will. I don't want the bitter cup. I don't want a crown of thorns. I don't want nails in My hands. I don't want nails in My feet. Nevertheless (Do you have a nevertheless in your prayers?), not My will but Thine be done" (see Matt. 26:39-42). Jesus, I see You as You leave the garden and the three disciples whom you trusted had let You down. They went to sleep in the prayer meeting, and you had to pray all by Yourself. I see Peter now as he wipes sleep from his eyes. I see James and John squinting, and I see John yawning. I hear You, Jesus, when you tell them, "Let's be going." But pretty soon here comes Judas. Judas had a name that meant treasure, but he was acting like trash. Judas, your name comes from Judea, and from the tribe of Judah, where the great kings came from. Judas, your name means treasure. It's a treasure because you are from the same tribe that the Messiah is from. You were meant to be treasure, but you're acting like trash.

I see you, Judas. You walk up and kiss Jesus, but you know you're lying because you've already sold Him out for thirty pieces of silver. Yes, you put a cheap price on heaven's best. You put a cheap price on the "Lily of the Valley," you put a cheap price on the Savior of the world. You can't buy salvation, but you want to sell it for the price of a slave. You want to devalue the treasure. But I'm so glad that the Treasure didn't mind. He took it for your sins and mine. He took it so I can stand here, so I can obey that spiritual that says, "Go, tell it on the mountain, over the hills and everywhere, that Jesus Christ is born." Judas sold You for thirty pieces of silver. But Your blood can't be paid for. Your blood reaches the highest mountain. Your blood reaches every generation. Your blood can save the lowest. I want to thank You, God. God said, "This is My beloved Son." Man said crucify Him. But His blood is the treasure. His blood is your treasure. His blood is my treasure.

My brothers and sisters, I want to ask you a question. Do you possess the Treasure within you? Now if you are outside of the church and you possess the Treasure, then you are depreciating its value. And so we extend the invitation to you today. First, of all to those who don't possess the Treasure, and second to those of you who knew about it sometime ago but somehow strayed away. We extend the invitation to you today. To those who need to come back and rededicate their lives, we extend the invitation to you and want you to know that's it's free to all who are willing to accept. Won't you come? This Treasure you don't have to buy with money.

JAS, Sr.

12
Tragedy of Wasted Treasures

Matthew 25:14-30

"Then the servants who had received one thousand coins came in and said, 'Sir, I know you are a hard man, you reap harvests where you did not plant, and you gather crops where you did not scatter seed. I was afraid, so I went off and hid your money in the ground'" (vv. 24-25, GNB).

If we were to step onto the balcony of time and look out over the theater of history, we would quickly observe that while history has brought vast technological advances, it has also led us to alarmingly high levels of wastefulness regarding the resources, blessings, and treasures created by God in the beginning. We are certainly a profligate generation. The once clear, clean air of creation has been polluted by petroleum fuel; which in its dwindling reserve has become a treasure of greed for which human blood has been wasted in the desert sands of the Middle East. The previously fresh-flowing streams and grand, glorious oceans of Genesis have been wasted and spoiled by technology's toxic waste, and by oil spills which destroy flora and fauna, as well as fish and fowl, which the Great Creator has entrusted to our dominion. "The Tragedy of Wasted Treasures."

The glistening, golden grain provided by God for the feeding of His people is now aborted by the few who dump their surplus rather than share with the hungry, hurting masses. Humankind, the jewel of creation, which God blessed to be in His own image, has been the most tragic of wasted treasure, as countless men and women have been destroyed by addiction to drugs and alcohol. It is a tragedy of human treasure, wasted and cast out upon the junk heaps of society. Throwaway children wander aimlessly on big-city streets, hungry for love as well as for food, while society looks the other way, refusing to notice the pain and sadness engraved in the faces of the little ones whom Jesus so deeply loves. Lip service is given by government to the importance of education, while government actions cut funds which would educate our youth and protect our treasured future. Human potential is wasted by humans—human intelligence wasted by humans, human talent wasted by humans, human creativity wasted, human vitality wasted, human strength wasted, human dreams, human aspirations—all wasted. Blessings of God, wasted, wasted, wasted, wasted. There is a horrible tragedy of wasted treasure.

God created such a wonderful world and entrusted us with the responsibility of taking care of it. However, we have been a generation of irresponsible stewards, a generation which has forgotten the voice of our Owner. Most seem to have utterly no recollection of the Owner. We are a generation containing some who even deny the existence of the Owner. This generation needs to be awakened to the fact that "The earth is the Lord's and the fullness thereof; the world, and they that dwell therein" (Ps. 24:1). God owns everything. Everything belongs to Him, and we are accountable.

Jesus warns us not to waste God's treasure as He relates the story which we commonly know as the parable of the three servants or the parable of the talents. In this parable a wealthy man prepared to leave home on a trip. Prior to leaving he entrusted his property to three servants, giving to each, according to ability. To one he gave five thousand coins, to another two thousand, and to a third, one thousand. When he returned he was happy to find that the first two servants had made investments to double the money entrusted to them. The property owner was saddened, however, to learn that the third servant had made no investment, but simply buried his coins in the ground. The servant had wasted the earning power of one thousand coins by making them buried treasure. A close look at the parable reveals that there are at least three reasons for the failure of this wasteful servant.

First:

This Servant Was Immobilized by Fear of His Master

He saw his master as a hard man who reaped where he did not plant and gathered crops where he did not scatter seed. This servant hid his master's coins because he was afraid of him. This fear was crippling. It created what has been termed "a paralysis of analysis." He was so busy analyzing what he saw as the hard, mean spirit of his master that he became paralyzed with fear. Some of us have been richly blessed by God with special talents, spiritual gifts, and material endowments. Yet we have allowed fear to "eat our lunch."

Fear convinces us to dig a hole and bury our gifts.

Fear has us second-guessing God's purpose for our lives.

Fear tricks us into seeing only problems and never opportunities.

Fear magnifies obstacles in our minds and diminishes the true size of our assets.

Fear has an elephant running from a mouse.

Fear has us seeing ourselves as grasshoppers and our enemies as giants. Fear is so destructive.

Fear will keep us from trying for a promotion on our job.

Fear will prevent a student from accepting a scholarship to a prestigious university in a distant state.

Fear will persuade us not to make a wise investment with surplus income.

Fear will stop us from becoming tithers when we know that God has blessed us beyond what we deserve.

Fear will dissuade us from serving the Lord as a worker in Sunday School, scouting, prison ministry, tutorial programs, evangelism, Big Brothers, or any of the many programs and ministries designed to help others.

Fear freezes our commitment and causes us to stand still while time passes us by.

Fear makes us apathetic, stagnant.

Fear stunts and ultimately stops our growth.

The first reason for the failure of the wasteful servant was fear. The second reason was:

This Servant Lacked Faith
As a Direct Result of Fear

The wasteful servant lacked faith in his master and faith in himself, lacked faith in the justice and fair play of his master, and lacked faith in his own ability to make prudent investments with the one thousand coins. Quite often we fail because of a lack of faith in God and a lack of faith in ourselves. Our lack of faith sees God not as a God of grace but as a God of stinginess. Our lack of faith views God not as a God of justice, but as a God of wrath. It regards God not as a helping friend but as a hindering foe. As a result, lack of faith in God creates a lack of faith in self, because faith in self is a by-product of faith in God.

When you have faith in God you know that you can do all things through Christ who strengthens you (see Phil. 4:13). When you have faith in God, you know that if God be for you, who can be against you? (see Rom. 8:31). When you have faith in God you know He will multiply your gifts as He multiplied the fish and loaves. If we are to be good stewards, we must affirm to ourselves that "God is able to make all grace abound toward you; That ye, always having all sufficiency in all things, may abound to every good work" (2 Cor. 9:8). His grace, His grace is sufficient. Have faith in God and you can climb high mountains. You can accomplish great things.

If you have faith as an individual God will enable you to accomplish personal goals. You will be His instrument for making your family a strong, loving, Christian family. If you have faith in God you will be strengthened to enhance your performance in your career. You will be able to better manage your personal finances and find resources for savings and investments. You will be able to improve the spiritual, mental, physical, and social aspects of life. You will be a stronger witness of Jesus Christ and a better serving Christian, giving to God the firstfruits through your talents, your time, and your tithes.

Yes, the first reason for failure on the part of the wasteful servant was fear. The second reason was the lack of faith. The third reason was:

This Servant Lacked Initiative

He failed to take the first step. The Scriptures inform us that while he hesitated, the first two servants went at once and invested the money. Oh, we have a problem with procrastination—putting off until tomorrow what could be easily done today. It is important, sisters and brothers, to take that first step. Take it while you're in motion. It's easier to get the second step moving if the first step is already in process. Don't we know that our equilibrium will force us into the second step if we are already into the first step? The laws of gravity are in our favor.

Procrastination is sometimes tied to fear and, if I can be so bold, at other times it is linked to laziness. I figure that it takes as much, if not more, energy to be lazy as it does to be productive. Laziness tires me out. Laziness makes me feel sluggish. If you make the first step, God will take the next. If you take the first step—I'm a witness—He'll take the next. We don't know oftentimes how that next step is going to be shaped, but God manages to find us firm footing for that second step. I've never found the second step to be a rocky step. I've never found that second step to be sinking sand, but always there is a place for me to put my foot because God makes a place for that second step. All He wants you to do, all He wants for me to do, is to just step. The second step will work itself out. The journey of a thousand miles begins with the first step.

The Issue in This Parable Was Not the Ability of the Servant

Yes, it does say that he gave to each according to ability, but you will notice that the second servant, who was not as able as the first servant, had a proportionate return, not an equal return on his investment, but a proportionate return. He received the same words of blessing from the master. It doesn't matter if you are a little less talented than the next person. God is not concerned about that. He is not going to discriminate against you because you've been a little less endowed than the person next to you.

God will bless whatever you do; if you do it you make an investment. He doesn't even require a proportionate return on your investment, because the Master said to the servant, "I didn't ask you to go and do some kind of slick investment scheme and over-multiply this money. You could have put the money in a bank and simply brought back some simple interest, and that would have satisfied me just as well. I still would have given you a blessing." Investing in the Lord's work is safe. God is not asking us to take unsafe risks. He's not asking you to take unsafe risks in your personal lives and unsafe risks with your family or unsafe risks in church. He could if He wanted to. He's merely saying, "Take what I give you and get the most out of it. Take what I give you and use it for the glory of the kingdom of God." We must push out of the block. We need to stop procrastinating. We need to forge ahead with the business of kingdom work.

Yes, it's time for us to move toward a conclusion. There were three problems that prevented success on the part of the wasteful servant. The first was *fear*. The second was *lack of faith*, and the third was *lack of inituitive*. Our wastefulness is almost childlike. I can remember when I was a little boy, my parents would work hard to provide for us. My father would take on a second job as a security guard or a janitor around Christmastime so he would be able to buy Christmas gifts for all five of his children. Good Christmas gifts. He and my mother worked hard. When we'd get those Christmas gifts you could see their joy on Christmas morning as our faces would light up with happiness. But I was wasteful because before New Year's Day would come around I would tear my toys up. Some of us have that kind of attitude when it comes to the blessings that God bestows upon us.

We look at our text. That wasteful steward allowed his lack of faith in his master and the resultant lack of faith in himself to stifle his potential as he buried his blessings. He permitted his fear to immobilize him, render him useless, and to rob him of his reward. He was truly a "Tragedy of Wasted Treasures." However, Jesus, the Giver of good news, shared that the two faithful servants were richly rewarded when the master repeated to each of them, "Well done, you good and faithful servants! . . . You have been faithful in managing small amounts, so I will put you in charge of large amounts. Come on and share my happiness!" (v. 21, GNB).

I'm so glad our Jesus is just that way. He loved to bless His servants. He loved us so much that He went to Calvary and suffered and died for us on an old rugged cross so we would be blessed with the treasure of eternal life—but He didn't stop there. No, no, no. On the third day He arose from the tomb with all power of heaven and earth in His hands. And that power, I tell you, is available to you and me today. I'm so glad that one day He's returning for His church, and when He returns He is going to summon all of His faithful servants. I want to hear Him say, "Well done, you've been a good steward of the gospel. You haven't buried it in the ground, but you have shared its saving power with persons lost and shattered by sin." I want to hear Him say, "Well done, you've been good and faithful stewards of hope. You've let your light so shine. You'd rather light a candle than curse the darkness. You have not hidden your light under a bushel, but you sat it on a hill so men and women, boys and girls would see your good works and glorify your Heavenly Parent." I want to hear Him say "Well done, you've been a good and faithful servant. You did not rob me. You brought all the tithes into the storehouse. Now I'll open the windows of heaven and pour you out a blessing that you shall not have room enough to receive it." I want to hear my Lord say, "Well done, good and faithful servant, you have not neglected the poor and oppressed."

"When they were hungry you fed them. When they were thirsty you gave them drink. When they were naked you clothed them.

When they were sick and in prison you visited them. When they were homeless you took them in. Come on now and inherit the kingdom I prepared for you from the foundation of the earth." I want to hear Him say, "Well done, you've done justly. You've loved mercy and you have walked humbly with thy God. Well done. You've loved Me with all your heart, with all your mind, and with all your soul. You've loved your neighbor as yourself. Well done. Well done. You've fought a good fight. You served Me with gladness. You've given with cheerfulness.

"You've prayed with fervor. You've worshiped God in spirit and in truth. Well done. You've listened to the lonely. You've encouraged the children. You've assisted the elderly. You've helped the homeless. Well done. You've befriended the friendless. You've hugged the hurting. You've visited the sick. Well done, you've blessed the bereaved. Enter now into the kingdom of heaven of your Lord."

JAS, Jr.

13
Where Is Your Weight?

Proverbs 3:5-10

In the *King James Version,* Proverbs 3:5-6 reads, "Trust in the Lord with all thine heart; and lean not unto thine own understanding. In all thy ways acknowledge him, and he shall direct thy paths." Verse 9 goes: "Honor the Lord with thy substance, and with the firstfruits of all thine increase." And verse 10 completes the thought. "So shall thy barns be filled with plenty, and thy presses shall burst out with new wine."

"Where Is Your Weight?" is not about whether you have too much weight exaggerated in certain portions of your body. That's not what I have in mind, Deacon Mackey. I'm talking in a spiritual sense rather than a physical sense. That should comfort some of us, who as we grow older, discover that our weight may be overexaggerated. I raise this question in a spiritual sense and suggest that your weight is your total self. It is your heart, It is your mind. It is your soul. It is your strength. It is the sum total of your emotional, mental, spiritual, and physical self. In fact, it is *all* of you. What is your weight? It is you, and if you have thrown all your weight on God, then you have obeyed Jesus who said, "Thou shalt love the Lord thy God with all thy heart, with all thy soul, and with all thy mind, and with all thy strength" (Matt. 12:30). But the next logical question is:

What Are You Doing with Your Weight?

Really, how are you using your weight? Where are you leaning with your weight? Where are you placing your weight? Is it on thin ice? Not too many years ago a group of seniors who were graduating from McClymonds High School decided to go up into the snow country to celebrate their graduation. Unfortunately, they did not return because they went out on a lake to ice-skate, but the ice was too thin to hold them up.

The text, "Lean not unto thine own understanding," is saying, "Don't place your faith on thin ice." "Lean not unto thine own understanding." You haven't lived long enough and if you had lived long enough, if you were the oldest person living in terms of time, that would not even be a grain of sand on the beach of eternity. That's why the writer of the Book of Proverbs says in 14:12, "There is a way that seemeth right unto a man, but the end thereof are the ways of death." A way that seems right. A way that seems right to man, to woman. It just seems right. But it's man's way that seems right. But the Bible says that "the end thereof are the ways of death." Human understanding merely seems right. Human understanding is on thin ice. When I think of *how* humans put their weight and *where* they put their weight, I discover that some put their weight on popularity, and that *seems* right. There is nothing lasting about popularity. Popularity changes just like clothing styles. Popularity changes just like hair styles. And so it seems right, but it isn't right.

Some put their weight on politics. I want you to know that merely seems right. It's thin ice. Politics change. Politicians come and go. Politicians don't always tell the truth. They can be against abortion, but if they get enough letters from their district saying, "we are for abortion," somehow the politicians change their positions and vote with the masses. I want something that's more reliable in my life than politics. I want Jesus, because the Book of Hebrews says that Jesus is "The same yesterday, and today, and for ever" (13:8). Some persons place their weight on status and power. But they may have those positions today, and tomorrow they may lose those positions for any illogical reasons. "God is our refuge and strength, a very present help in trouble" (Ps. 46:1).

Economic power seems right, so many people place their faith in the financial pages of the newspapers. Their sermons are the stock-market reports of news commentators. These persons are walking on thin ice instead of trusting God. Trust God who is not temperamental like the weather. You may choose someone to be your friend, and you will want to lean on them for security, but they may be temperamental. Today they may love you, but next week they may choose the crowd that doesn't love you. You need Jesus, "The same yesterday, and today, and for ever." Jesus isn't thin ice. He is the Rock. He multiplies fish and loaves. When you don't think you are going to have enough in your kitchen, somehow He takes five barley loaves and two small fish and multiplies them.

Place your weight on God, the Sure Foundation. Let God hold you up. Trust Him. Acknowledge Him. God will direct your steps, your paths. God is your Counselor, your Conductor, your Copilot. God wishes to manage your life. "Lean not unto thine own understanding." Your own understanding is thin ice. Let God be the traffic manager of your daily life. The traffic policeman stands there and holds out one hand and tells you when to stop. When you have stopped long enough, he beckons you forward with another hand. "In all thy ways acknowledge Him and He will give you a caution light. Then He'll tell you to wait awhile, and then when you don't need to wait any longer, He will give you the green light. Jesus is my Traffic Policeman. Jesus is my Light. For God will supervise your walk. In all thy ways acknowledge Him, and He will direct thy walk. He will direct thy path, and all of us need our walk directed. You know the choir used to sing a song, "We'll walk in the light, beautiful light, Come where the dewdrops of mercy are bright, . . . Jesus, the light of the world." He will supervise your walk because Jesus is the Light of the world.

God will supervise your work of love. God is love. Some of us may work in the church but sometimes we work complaining, grumbling, finding fault, and criticizing, but our work ought to be in love. The Bible says, "Whatsoever ye do, do all to the glory of God" (1 Cor. 10:31). Do it, not to the honor of your pastor. Do it, not to the satisfaction of your ego, but in the spirit of love. If you don't do it in the spirit of love, though you give your body to be burned, though you speak with the tongues of men and of angels, yes, it is a sounding brass and a tinkling cymbal (see 1 Cor. 13:1-2).

Without love it's thin ice, I tell you. It won't hold you up in the judgment day. It won't hold you up when the world's on fire. God will supervise. He will direct your path. Lean not to your own understanding. Don't put your weight on what you think but on the mind of Christ. Don't put your weight on how you see it. How you see it doesn't count. You can't see far enough. Put your weight on God. God will manage your work of love, your walk in the light. God will supervise your worship, your walk, your work, your ways—your walk in the light, your work in peace and in harmony, your ways of glory to God. But God will also supervise your worship of honoring Jesus. You ought to be in church not to look around to see who's there, not to see what somebody else is wearing, not because this is a fashion show, but to worship, praise, and honor the Lord. Your weight ought to honor God. Your weight is all of your heart, all of your mind, all of your soul, and all of your strength honoring God.

The *Good News Bible* says, "Honor the Lord by making him an offering from the best" (Prov. 3:9). But I was born and bred on the *King James Version*. So let me go back to it. The *Kings James Version* says, "Honor the Lord with thy substance, and with the firstfruit of all thine increase." That means when that Bible was translated, it was written in an agricultural community. So when the first crop came in, before you took your part you gave God His part. But we don't believe in doing it like that. We take our part *first*, but yet the Lord gave it to us. And then we give everybody else their part *next*, and if there's any left, God gets His part. And yet we don't feel guilty in repeating, "Thou shalt love the Lord thy God with all thy heart, and with all thy soul, and with all thy mind." "If I honor God with giving from off the top, then, Brother Preacher, will I have enough to live off of from the bottom?" Who gave you the top, the middle, and the bottom? Didn't you say He woke you up this morning and started you on your way? Didn't you say that He clothed you in your right mind and gave you the activity of your body parts?

It seems to me that He deserves the firstfruits. He deserves gifts from off the top. Who gave you your substance? Who continues to give you your substance? Who gave you the ability to earn your substance? If your answer is God, then why not honor Him before you pay your house note? Before you pay your rent? Before you pay your car payment, your insurance, your food, your water, your lights, and your heating bill? If you believe that God is, if you believe that God has blessed you, if you believe that God has provided for you, if you believe the integrity of the Holy Bible, if you believe that God said what He meant and meant what He said when He said, "Honor the Lord, . . . with the firstfruits of [your substance]," why didn't you put God first? Some of us build our budget the wrong way. You can't tithe because you didn't start out right. You started out paying *everybody*. God was an afterthought, and what you had left you gave to Him. But we ought to reorder our thinking.

The church needs to be converted. We talk about converting those in prison. We talk about converting the folks on drugs. We need to be converted in the sense of changing our own thinking. We need to change some of our attitudes. We need to get rid of some of our alibis, sit down, and hear the Word of the Lord. When J. Alfred is dead, God's Word will live on. When they have forgotten about this generation, God's Word will live on.

"The grass withereth, the flower fadeth: but the word of our God shall stand forever" (Isa. 40:7-8). The Scripture says, "Honor the Lord, . . . with thy firstfruits." Where is your weight? Do you really trust God to keep His promises to provide for you? I'm wondering if we do not have a faith problem. I'm wondering if we really have faith in the Lord. If you have faith in God, then you will lean on Him. If you really have faith in God you will do what His Word says—and then lean on Him to make a way out of no way. If you truly have faith in the Lord you will lean on Him. Lean on Him and see if He won't do what He says. If you have faith in the Lord, lean on Him and see if He will open doors for you and see if He won't fight your battles and if He won't part the raging sea. Lean on Him, lean on Jesus. Lean on the Everlasting Arms. We'll have power if we only lean on Him.

At Calvary, God put weight on His Son, Jesus. Put weight on Jesus. And Jesus carried that weight. "All we like sheep have gone astray; we have turned every one to his own way" (Isa. 53:6). Every now and then our church gets too big for me, and I realize I can't fix everything that's "broke" in this church, but I give it back to Jesus. It belongs to Him. I put the weight on Jesus. Because it says, "Upon this rock I will build my church" (Matt. 16:18). Sometimes my problems become so heavy. Yes, Mama became ill, JoAnna got sick. Problems to the left, problems to the right. I just needed a comforting word. Couldn't find it. I had to go straight to Jesus and simply lean on Him. You do that, too.

JAS, Sr.

14
When You Are Too Tired to Go Any Further

Isaiah 40:27-31

Verse 30 of Isaiah 40 reads, "Even those who are young grow weak; young men can fall exhausted" (GNB). How many of you have ever been so tired you felt you just couldn't go any further? I have been there many times.

There are so many situations and circumstances that tire us; so many matters that cause our spirits to become weary; so many problems that discourage us and sap our spirits. How many times have you found yourself asking, "If it's not one thing it's another"? "When it rains, it pours." "Lord, when will it ever end?" "Lord, have mercy." So many pains confront us, surround us, and immerse us to tire us out. Sometimes it's physical tiredness we experience, tiredness because we've been toiling too hard, tiredness because we work our knuckles to the bone, and we are "tilling the soil" with sweat-drenched brows, and we are plain physically tired. And sometimes physical tiredness doesn't come because we've worked so hard, but because somehow nature has dealt us the hand of sickness. Sometimes we just don't feel strong because our blood pressure is high or diabetes has weakened us. Sometimes we are not strong, and we are tired because we have been lying on our backs ill with illness we didn't select, illness not of our own choosing. Perhaps we are lying on our backs, can't get up, and we wish that we could. Many have debilitating illnesses; others have serious illnesses that doctors feel may be terminal. People who were once robust men and women now find themselves down to mere skin and bones, weakened, frail. They cry out or either think or whisper the words, *Lord, I am just too tired. I can't go any further. Too tired, too tired, I can't move one more step. Too tired, I can't even lift my arms. Too tired, I can't even open my eyelids. I'm just too tired to go any further.*

If it's not a physical sickness which tires our spirits; if we've been blessed with strength physically; if we have been blessed so we are able physically to exercise or work out at a gym, then we may find that we become emotionally tired. Maybe we are tired because conditions surrounding us wear us out, tired because our important relationships are so strained that we want to "throw in the towel." "My husband doesn't understand me." "My wife doesn't understand me." "Lord, I do all You tell me to do. I pray, and I provide for my children, but I just can't get them to do the right thing. I am tired. I'm throwing up my hands in frustration. Lord, I can't go any further with these relationships." It tires us out, causes us to bow our heads under the weight of emotional fatigue.

If we don't experience that kind of fatigue in intimate relationships, the relationships relating to our survival just tire us out. "Lord, I'm tired of this dead-end job. Every time there is an opportunity for promotion I get passed by. I'm just tired. This is leading nowhere. I'm tired of people picking on me. I'm tired of dealing with an immoral, unethical supervisor. I got into this work because I thought I could do some good, but, Lord, all I am doing is shuffling papers. All I am doing, Lord, is carrying out activities that don't add to anything in the grand scheme of things. I'm tired. I can't go another step. I'm tired, and I'm locked in because I've lost my self-confidence. I can't leave this job and go to another job. I'm getting older, Lord. I can't branch out. They are not going to hire a person my age somewhere else and pay me what I am used to getting. I'm tired."

And then those of us who are fortunate to be blessed with physical strength and have supportive relationships around us, fortunate enough to go to work, and have a little peace on the job and feel that there is some self-actualization occurring, find ourselves saddened, weakened, and weary because we cannot ignore the conditions of humanity, of our people, and of the world. We can't close our eyes and not notice that a war went on, using high-tech military equipment, a war that had people marching in the streets victoriously. Somehow it was not a war that ended neatly because refugees were crowded along the edges of the Iraqi border. Saddam Hussein is still in power. We are uneasy, because as we worship God there is turmoil and hatred around the world. Our black brethren in South Africa are still not free. Let us pray that they will be. "Let freedom ring." There is oppression all over the world—yes, even here in "the land of the free and the home of the brave."

It makes us tired when we understand that our foreparents labored for generations for a better world for us, for freedom, and racism still exists. Hate crimes still exist. Bigotry still exists. Discrimination still exists. The Nazis still march. The Klan still convenes. It makes you kind of tired, and makes you wonder why we are losing economically. I'm not merely talking about the fact that the gross national product has dipped drastically. I'm talking about the fact that we are suffering where the rubber meets the road in our day-to-day existence. Joblessness is rampant. Young people still are full of rage, hopelessness, and despair because they don't see what they are going to school for. They don't see a place waiting for them when they finish school. It makes you kind of tired, so tired you wonder if there is any reason to go any further.

We find ourselves joining in as a choral response, echoing the words of Fannie Lou Hamer, the great civil rights leader: "I'm sick and tired of being sick and tired. Sick and tired of being sick and tired because I've been tired a long time, and things don't seem to be getting any better. Sick and tired because I've been tired a long time, and I don't see any dividends coming in on my investments." As we ponder the nature of our weariness, as we look at this context of suffering and emotional, spiritual, and physical fatigue, I discover myself doing what I always do—looking to the Word of God for help. In the Word of God I will find some insight. In the Word of God I will find a solution. I will discover in the Word of

God meaning and purpose to the seemingly unending avalanche of human suffering.

And as I have passed through this process of spiritually seeking the Word of God, I have found myself directed to two passages of Scripture—one in the Old Testament, a second in the New Testament. One passage is the ever-popular piece of poetry found in Isaiah 40, and the second passage is the familiar piece of instruction, penned by Paul in 2 Corinthians 4. Yes, both of these texts help us deal with the issue of suffering and our weariness. Both of these texts help us to realize what we must do when we feel too tired to go any further.

First:

These Texts Describe the Nature of Our Weary Condition

In the 27th verse of Isaiah 40, we are informed that our condition is related to our feeling of being ignored by God. In that verse the writer cries pathetically, "Israel, why do you complain that the Lord doesn't know your troubles or care if you suffer injustice?" (GNB). That, my sisters and brothers, indicates that when we are encountering trouble there is a relationship between our sense of closeness to God and our condition of suffering. There is also a direct correlation when we are not suffering.

I would then surmise that we feel somehow closer to God, and when we are suffering we often feel farther from God. If we are suffering a lot, we somehow feel a lot farther from God. That's the way, at least, the Old Testament Israelites interpreted their own suffering. Their suffering had to do with the fact that they felt distant from God. Some would explain that the sense of distance was predicated upon the fact that their suffering was based upon sin. Paul lets us know it is not necessarily a cause of relationship. Hence we must state, though, that when we are spiritually fatigued (according to the Israelites), when we feel that we are all alone, we are most tired. When we feel the greatest distance from God we find ourselves asking the questions, "Lord, where are you? Where are you, Lord, as I go through trials and tribulations?

Lord, if you are a God of justice, how can You stand by and watch me be treated this way? Lord, if You are truly concerned about me, and are not some sadistic God of creation, certainly you must stop injustice from occurring."

Though we are removed from the Old Testament, sisters and brothers, we join in with those ancient people with our attitudes. When we are hurting, we wonder, "Where is the Lord?" I've been there. I remember being in the hospital the first week that I served here as assistant pastor. For some reason I was put in the hospital, and Dr. Scott came by and said, "We're taking some tests. We don't know exactly what the situation is." And I asked, "Doc, am I going to have to stay here?"

And he replied, "I don't know.

And I began to cry. "I ain't going to die, am I?" I cried. I broke down. Dr. Scott looked at me with his eyebrows raised and put it to me, "Reverend, you need to pray to that God you've been telling us about." We sometimes feel distant from God. We feel that God may not understand or does not hear us. Why would you ignore us, God? The worst part of our suffering is the sense of being estranged from God. Job had all of those maladies, all of those problems. He could have dealt with those problems, but the one fact he couldn't deal with was that God wouldn't speak to him during that period.

These Texts Indicate Our Condition

The second indication of our condition is also shared in Isaiah. Isaiah lets us know that the young men shall be fatigued; even they shall lose their strength, and shall become wearied, utterly exhausted. This point made by Isaiah, I think, has special pertinence to us today, because when I look at our community it seems that the most weary, the most tired are those who are physically the strongest! Go to Santa Rita with Reverend Stephens and you will see men who have pumped a lot of weight and have big bulky bodies who are tired, who have given up. They are more tired than the elders who are sitting in the pews. I believe the reason for that tiredness is because they have lost the sense of their sacred history. That's why Isaiah says, "Do you not know? Were you not told a long time ago? Have you not heard how the world began?" (v. 21, GNB). Didn't your parents tell you about God and about His power, and about His majesty? Don't you know about your sacred history? Don't you know about God who delivered Daniel, the God who delivered your ancestors who had to travel perilous middle passages? He is God who somehow stood by your foreparents as they were chained and shackled and allowed them to survive, with their heads "screwed on tight" and surviving with a good, wholesome view of life that is not taken down by bitterness and by defeatism. Don't you know anything about that God? Don't you have any connections with your sacred history?

Quite often, sisters and brothers, we embellish and exacerbate our suffering condition and become more tired and more weary because we lose contact with our sacred history. Can't we remember that He brought us thus far by faith? Leaning on Him He has brought us. Can't we remember that stony road we trod, the bitter chastening rod, in the days when hope was unborn. Can't we remember that we made it through those days? Can't we remember the God of our weary years, the God of our silent tears? Can't we remember? We become cut off, separated, disconnected, dislocated from our sacred history. Being in that condition we become even more weary.

Strong, robust young men who have everything to live for suddenly just give up. They suddenly allow their dreams to become deferred. So our condition is described most adequately by Isaiah.

As we move on I want to tell you that Paul also describes our condition. In 2 Corinthians 4:8-9 he says, "We are often troubled, . . . sometimes in doubt." He tells us that "there are many enemies" and that we are "badly hurt." That's the condition we find ourselves in. It's a desperate condition of trouble, of hurt, a condition of having enemies in our midst. But the apostle Paul tells us that we have to put these troubles into perspective. He doesn't merely say that we are troubled; he says "We are often troubled, but not crushed; sometimes in doubt, but never in despair; there are many enemies, we are never without a friend; and though badly hurt at times, we are not destroyed" (GNB).

I must share with you, sisters and brothers, that though our condition may look bad, it is not a lost one. We must put our condition in perspective. Some of us have lost that perspective. We have taken our condition out of proportion and have magnified it so it immobilizes us. Yes, we have troubles, but we are not destroyed. You may feel weak, and the doctors may have told you your illness is terminal, but I want you to recognize you need to put that condition into perspective. To live is Christ and to die is gain (see Phil. 1:21). Jesus has gone to prepare a place for us, that where He is there may we also be (see John 14:2-3). Put your condition into perspective. Whatever your problem is, it's not a problem of defeat. It may look bad, but it's not a lost situation. Let's put our conditions into perspective.

Then Paul lets us know that, even when we are in contact with God and even when we have our perspective in focus, we still suffer. We may have a sense of sacred history, but we still suffer— but all is not lost. We haven't suffered in vain. The ultimate victory lies ahead. He puts our situation into perspective. Not only is our condition revealed in our text, but:

These Texts Reveal the Purpose for Our Condition

I didn't say a reason for our condition. I stated there is purpose for our condition, not our purpose, but God's purpose. I become tired of hearing people saying, "Yes, I know that this catastrophe happened because God wanted me to see this or to see that. There is a reason for this and for that and God did it for my benefit." I have problems with that. I watched a guy on television who was a survivor of an air crash, who changed his ticket at the last moment and didn't get on the plane. He said, "Yes, I was spared, and the reason that this whole thing happened was because God was trying to tell me something." God allowed 150 people to fall out of the air and die only to give that man a message. That's bad theology, sisters and brothers. "God took this child from me because He was trying to get a message through to me. My purpose. The purpose is for me." No, no, no, that's bad theology. There is purpose to our suffering, but it is not *our* purpose, it's *God's* purpose. Now we may fit into His purpose, but the purpose is much bigger than we are. The purpose has a divine justice to it, and so those people who fell out of the air and died in that crash somehow are taken care of in God's sublime purpose. The little child who was taken from mom and pop fits into God's purpose. The child benefits from God's purpose. It's not a self matter for you or me. It's God's purpose, and that's what Paul meant on another occasion when he said, "Yes, God's purpose is involved in everything. All things work together for good to them that love God, to them who are the called according [not to my purpose, not for your purpose] to His purpose" (see Rom. 8:28).

Purpose has meaning. Purpose is greater than reasons. They could be good or bad reasons, but purpose involves God's goal, God's intentionality, God's aim, and His aim is always to reconcile the world to Himself. There is purpose to our condition. The supreme purpose belongs to God. The supreme will is God's, and everything that is supreme is God's. That is what we need to understand. The supreme power belongs to God. It's not our power, but the supreme power is His. Sometimes we forget that God is in charge. And if He put us—not in clay pots which could suffer, which are frail, and which are fragile, but in golden vessels—we'd start admiring how we look in the mirror and trying to assess our value on the external, not recognizing that the true value is not outside, but what's inside. The spiritual treasure is inside of the clay vessel. That is why we go through suffering. We go through it to show that the supreme power belongs to God and not to us.

Verses 10 and 11 tell us that we carry in our bodies the death of Jesus, so His life may be seen in our mortal bodies. That's another purpose. As we suffer, we join Christ in His sufferings and those with whom we come in contact will see within us Jesus, alive and incarnate. That's why we suffer. It is God's purpose, not our own purpose. But God doesn't stop with simply describing conditions, with just talking about the *purpose* of this condition, but:

These Texts Express Coping with Our Condition

The first step we must take, according to Isaiah, is to recognize that God created all things. We must recognize God, who is full of grace and majesty, who is omnipotent, who is worthy of our praise and glory. We have to recognize God. When we recognize God, then we are able to cope better with our sufferings.

Second, Isaiah tells us that if we are going to be able to cope with our sufferings, if we want to be relieved of our sufferings, we must wait on the Lord. Some of us become very rash and want to take things into our own hands. Some of us would run into an army of bazookas, grenades, and missile launchers with a pocketknife and move recklessly. But God says, "Wait on Me. Don't move rashly. You are immobilized. You are tired. You can't move any further. Well, then, I'm not going to ask you to move. Just wait on Me. Just sit there. It's all right for you feel like you can't go any further. Wait on Me."

Coach Clifton, when I went to Portola Junior High they had an event called the Turkey Trot, which happened right before Thanksgiving, and we junior high kids would run a race, and the winner would receive the turkey. I knew I wasn't going to win the turkey. All of the fast guys and all of the "cool" guys were running in this race. I was a lousy sprinter, so I kept trying to run that 50- and 100-yard dash, but I never ran anything that was over a mile long. I was running in the race, got tired, and said, "Lord, have mercy on me. I'm not going to be able to go very far in this race." I kept on running a little bit more, and before I knew it my ankles became heavy. I was really tired, my lungs started drying out, and I said, "Oh, Lord." You could look at me and see that I was struggling and had lost stride. I couldn't move.

I wasn't in shape to run the distance, but my pride kept me going because all of those guys were popular. They were up front, styling, kicking, reaching out. They were gone, so I kind of hung in

there, and guess what. When I came near that straightaway, something miraculous happened. I found something in time, and I was
able to kick, kick, and kick, and I started passing up runners.
There were about 100 young fellows running in that race, and I
didn't win. I came in eighth place, but I didn't understand what
was going on. So I went over to the coach, Coach Rodick. I said,
"Coach, I can't explain what happened. I was so tired out, and I'm
not tired now. But, man, I was really tired." He turned around and
said, "Well, young man, that's what we call the second wind."

I tell you, just wait on the Lord. He'll give you a second wind. I
don't know what your trouble may be, but if you wait on the Lord
He will give you a second wind. You'll be able to run that race. You
may not come in as quickly as you want to, but you will make it if
you will wait on the Lord. He may not come when you ask Him to
come, but He is always right on time. You know what happens if
you wait on the Lord, and you don't fix your attention on the
things that you can see.

When I was running that race, Coach, I had to block the trees out
of those mountains, I had to block the incline, because the incline
would have tired me out further. I had to block everything out of
my view and move it to my subconscious, and deal with my
spirituality, and that's when I hit that second wind. I found myself
doing what Paul says. When you block out the things which are
seen and focus on the things that are unseen, you'll make it
through.

I don't know about you today, but I'm not going to focus on the
trials and tribulations we all face. I'm not going to focus in on the
hindrances that work to prevent our movement. I'm not going to
focus in on negativity coming from the next guy. I'm not going to
be discouraged by the negative, but "I don't feel no ways tired. I've
gone too far from where I started from. No, no, no, I don't feel no
ways tired. Nobody told me the road would be easy." I don't
believe that the Lord brought me this far to leave me here. "I don't
feel no ways tired." I'm going to keep on running the race. I'm
going to run on until I get my second wind. Trouble, don't bother

me. I'm going to run on. Satan, get out of my way. I'm going to keep on running. "I don't feel no ways tired."

Don't give up. Keep on running. Don't get discouraged. Keep on going strong. Before Deacon Sellers moves on I've got to share something with you here. From time to time I just become so discouraged. I get tired sometimes of going to hospitals and seeing young people, good people, probably much better people than I, find them on their death beds. I get tired of going with Reverend Stephens to the jailhouse and seeing good, young people there who made a mistake and are paying for it. I get tired of it. Sometimes I feel like what they refer to as "a wounded healer," trying to bring comfort to everybody else.

The other night my father called me from Chicago. He said, "Son, I sense you are tired, sense that you are frustrated." He said, "Son, I want to direct you to 2 Corinthians, fourth chapter." The Holy Spirit didn't give me that text directly. He sent the text through the pastor to me. And you know, I've read that text many times, and I have dealt with the theological implications of that text. I have dealt with the logic of that text. I've dealt with the metaphorical usage of language in that text. But there is something about the Word of God which goes beyond words, beyond logical meaning. This time when I read the text, the text moved inside of me and started healing, gave me strength, and chased the fog from my eyes so I can see more clearly.

The Word of God works like that. I challenge you not to let the logic of this text deal with your intellect, but let the power of the text move within your heart. I guarantee you: if you do it, it will heal you; if you do it, it will give you strength to go forward. I can't speak to your individual conditions today, but I am aware that there is something weighing down each one of us. Let that text move into your heart. God will give you victory. Yes, He will. "I don't feel no ways tired."

Some of us may feel too tired to go any further, but we have heard a word from the Lord and know that there is a second wind. I invite you right now to take the second wind. Maybe you have walked with the Lord for a time, but you have slowed down and are too tired to go any further. Come on and take your second wind.

JAS, Jr.

15
Bouncing Back from Defeat

John 21:15-22

Introduction

All of us know what it means to experience defeat. All of us have gone through setbacks and hurts. We all have had disappointments and disasters; calamities and catastrophes. We know what it feels like to be sick and in bed under the doctor's care. We know the pain of bereavement. We know what it's like to be humiliated and shamed or to have our hearts broken. Yes, we know what it is like to experience defeat. Just listen to the many and varied voices of defeat:

1. "Ever since my wife died, I've been a wreck. I can't break out of this depression."
2. "My husband left me, and I can't pick up the pieces."
3. "My job is a living hell. I dread getting up in the morning and going to work."
4. "I knew it was a small risk, but I didn't expect to lose everything."
5. "I've done some rotten things in my life and I just can't forgive myself."
6. "I let my family down, I let myself down, and I let God down."
7. "Yeah, I made a mistake. I wish I could turn back the clock and correct it, but I can't."
8. "Grown-ups think that children don't worry about anything, but they're wrong. I worry about school, I worry about my report card, and I worry about failure."

9. "It's rough being a teenager. I have no one to talk to; I mean, really talk to about my problems. My parents are good people, but they just don't understand. I'm lonely."

10. "I started drinking socially. Now I can't quit, yet I hate alcohol."

Everyone of us knows about hardship and humiliation. We've been emotionally whipped. We've been "clobbered" by life. We have had downfalls and nosedives. We've been conquered and crushed, overwhelmed and undone. We've been broken and battered, shaken and shattered. We've known fiascoes and failures. We've been in messes and misfortunes, and with our misdeeds we have missed the mark.

This, my sisters and brothers, is the nature of the human condition. But we are not the only ones who have experienced defeat. The Word of God tells us about the troublesome experience of a man named Peter. Peter speaks to us through the tunnel of history.

Thank you, Peter. We can relate to your sense of shame and defeat. All have sinned and come short of the glory of God. Oh, yes, Peter, we can empathize with your predicament. We know that when we would do good, evil is all around us. Tell us, Brother Peter, what did you do to begin the process of bouncing back from defeat?

Peter: "I communed with the Lord. After Jesus was resurrected, He made several appearances to those of us who loved Him. On one occasion He appeared to me and the other disciples while we were fishing. After filling our nets with fish, He summoned us to sup with Him. That meal for me was more than just eating food for my body. That meal provided me with an opportunity to commune with the Lord. I was able to share my sense of hurt with Him. Our minds communed, our spirits communed, my soul communed with the Lord."

Thank you, Peter.

Sisters and brothers, according to Peter, the first step for us to take, if we want to bounce back from defeat, is to commune with the Lord. That means, when we fall on hard times we need to: "Have a little talk with Jesus and tell him all about our troubles."

When we have problems, some of us talk to everybody in the world but Jesus. We tell people who aren't interested and don't want to be bothered. We tell people who listen politely and when we are gone they laugh at us, or shake their heads in disgust, and then go and put all our business in the streets. When you have a problem, tell Jesus! When you're hurting, tell Jesus! When burdens are weighing you down, tell Jesus! When your enemies are making your life miserable, tell Jesus! When you are confused or discouraged, tell Jesus! When you can't look at yourself in the mirror because of shame, tell Jesus! When your own sin won't let you sleep at night, tell Jesus!

Elisha Hoffman wrote it well: "I must tell Jesus, all of my trials; / I cannot bear these burdens alone; / I must tell Jesus, all of my troubles; / . . . Jesus can help me, Jesus alone."

When we are experiencing defeat, let's do like Peter and commune with the Lord. Sisters and brothers, you have often heard my father and me share how sad we feel when members who are hurting decide in their suffering to stay away from church. It's during painful days that we most need to be in the house of the Lord. It's during these times that God speaks to us through the preached Word. It's during these painful moments that the Holy Spirit will minister to us through the anointed singing of this choir. It's during our sorrow that we need to be at the altar when prayer is lifted up, providing us a glimpse of heaven. Yes, in our hour of defeat we need to commune with the Lord. Jesus said, "Behold, I stand at the door, and knock: if any man hear my voice, and open the door, I will come in to him, and will sup with him, and he with me" (Rev. 3:20). Well, let's check back with Peter.

Brother Peter, tell us what else occurred to help you bounce back from defeat.

Peter: "Jesus asked me, point-blank, if I loved Him. I told Him I did. He then ordered me to feed His sheep. Then He asked me again and again. Three times He asked me that question, and I told Him I loved Him every time. And every time He told me to feed His sheep, that really disturbed me. I wanted to know why He had to ask me three times. I know that the Lord is not hard of hearing. Then it occurred to me; He wants me to make this affirmation three times to nullify the three times that I had earlier denied Him. Well, let me say it again—I love Jesus and I shall ever feed His sheep. I want you who live in the twentieth century to know this simple truth: if you serve the Lord you will bounce back from defeat."

Brother Peter, that's really profound. If we serve the Lord we will bounce back from defeat.

Sisters and brothers, let's take a look at how that works. The Lord told Peter three times that if he loved Him to feed His sheep. Peter was hurting. Don't tell me that the Lord did not come in and pat him on the back and talk sympathetically to him. Instead of massaging Peter's wounds, the Lord ordered Peter back onto the field of play, "Feed My sheep, get up from the seat of self-pity, and follow. There's work to be done. I want you to serve Me." That's how you bounce back from defeat.

Sisters and brothers, we are hurting with a variety of ailments, but if we want to bounce back from defeat we are going to have to serve the Lord. Every one of us can be an evangelist of good news. The pastor was sharing with me about one of our good brothers who is in a lot of pain with multiple sclerosis, yet this brother is doing a marvelous job with a ministry of encouragement. He writes letters to public figures, and he gives them supportive words of encouragement. His letters give strength to leaders who don't hear encouragement from the community. That's good news. That's letting your light shine.

When you serve the Lord, goodness will come out of your work. People who are helped will find jobs, and their jobs will come back to you. Tell good news, do good news, and be good news. When you tell good news to others, you end up hearing good news yourself, if you listen to yourself talk. When you *do* good news, not only do others benefit, but *you* benefit. Every time I pray for someone else I am helped because I'm brought into the presence of the Lord. I cannot count the number of times I have visited sick persons in hospitals and left with more blessings than they received from me. It pays to serve Jesus. If you would be a messenger of good news, if you would be a witness for our Lord, you will find that productivity takes your mind off your problems. Some of us get so wrapped up in our problems that we magnify them in our minds beyond their importance. We end up making a mountain out of a molehill. We end up worrying about something that's not worth the effort. Our minds are on failure instead of on faith. We've got our minds on panic instead of prayer, on worry instead of on winning, on sorrow instead of on service. An idle mind is the devil's workshop. When you serve the Lord, you don't have time to worry. When you serve the Lord you can bounce back from defeat.

You'll find new strength, new joy, and new hope. He'll give you a new attitude, a new lease on life. "Oh, I keep so busy serving my Jesus, if I don't serve Him, the rocks are going to cry out, ain't got time to die!"

1. It still hurts that my wife is dead, but the Lord gives me strength and there is so much joy in serving Him.

2. I'm a single mother, but Jesus heads my household. I'm satisfied and complete, and I'm going to be His witness to other women who feel abandoned.

3. Sure, my job was a headache, but through serving Jesus, I've discovered new fulfillment which allows me to be His witness even on the job. And do you know what? Work is a lot less stressful now.

4. Yes, I'm broke, but Jesus has given me the inspiration to reconstruct my life. I'm not materialistic anymore. I feel wealthy by serving the Lord.

5. It's true that I used to be a rotten scoundrel, but I confessed to the Lord, and now He is using me for His glory to lead others to Jesus Christ and His saving grace.

6. I've discovered that when I lift up the name of Jesus, He picks me up and makes me glad. It makes my family glad, and it makes the Lord glad. There is victory in His name.

7. Yes, I made a bad mistake but I know now that God forgives me so I feel good about myself and I'm going to serve the Lord.

8. Jesus helps me not to worry. If I do my best, that's all He expects of me.

9. Since I met Jesus I now have a friend to talk to all the time.

10. I used to fill up on alcohol, and I never got enough. Now I fill up on Jesus, and "my cup runneth over."

Well, we've discovered that the formula for bouncing back from defeat involves: (1) communing with the Lord, and (2) serving the Lord.

But something still seems to be missing. Hmm, let's call Peter again. Hey, Brother Peter!

Peter: "What is it? Why is it that you twentieth-century preachers think you must always have three points to every sermon? I thought you were going to extend the invitation."

I'm sorry, Peter, but something is still missing. Here it is. It's right here in the Word. In verse 18 Jesus said to you, "I am telling you the truth; when you were young, you used to get ready and go anywhere you wanted to; but when you are old, you will stretch out your hands and someone else will tie you up and take you where you don't want to go" (GNB). Then the Gospel writer goes on to report that when Jesus said that to you, Peter, He was telling you that you were going to die from crucifixion and, in that way, bring glory to God. Now, how does that fit into your bouncing back from defeat?

Peter: "I'm so glad you asked that. Suffering while serving Jesus is the ultimate victory. I can say that now, because with the knowledge of how I would die, I yet never relented in the service of my Lord, not after the risen Savior appeared to me that day. He enabled me to preach the gospel with vigor and joy from that day forward. You remember how I preached on Pentecost? The Lord blessed that day. Yes, I served with gladness. You remember later how I laid my hands on Tabitha, and the Lord raised her from the dead? Or the time when Aeneas was healed of palsy? It pays to serve Jesus. The Lord later gave me a vision wherein He communicated to me that there are no persons who are exempted from His grace; so I led Cornelius, the Gentile, to Christ. When my day came, when my journey was over, like my Lord, crucifixion awaited me on an old, rugged cross. I could say, like Paul, 'I have fought a good fight, I had finished my course, I had kept the faith.' (see 2 Tim. 4:7). If you serve the Lord, your suffering is not defeat, your suffering is victory."

You said it well, Peter. If you serve Jesus He'll turn your scars into stars. He'll turn your cross into a crown. If we will be His disciples, He told us, "Lo I am with you always, even unto the end of the world" (Matt. 28:20). He will be with us as we encounter dangers seen and unseen. He'll be with us in our tears of the midnight hour and during the disappointment of dreams deferred. He'll comfort us during the thunderous storms of life and will warm us during the cold winters of despair. He'll walk with us down rocky roads and talk to us in lonely abodes. He will be with us. He will strengthen us. His grace is sufficient.

I decided to follow Jesus; No turning back, no turning back. If God be for us, who can be against us? I have decided to follow Jesus. No turning back, no turning back.

For we know [that whatever our troubles may be] "that all things work together for good to them that love God, to them who are the called according to his purpose" (Rom. 8:28). I have decided to follow Jesus, No turning back, no turning back.

"In all these things we are more than conquerors through him that loved us" (v. 37). "For I am persuaded, that neither death, nor life, nor angels, nor principalities, nor powers, nor things present, nor things to come, Nor height, nor depth, nor any other creature, shall be able to separate us from the love of God, which is in Christ Jesus, our Lord" (v. 38).

"I am persuaded that he is able to keep that which I have committed unto him against that day" (2 Tim. 1:12). I have decided to follow Jesus; No turning back, no turning back. "To live is Christ, and to die is gain" (Phil. 1:21). "Oh death, where is thy sting? O grave, where is thy victory?" (1 Cor. 15:55).

"For our light affliction, which is but for a moment, worketh for us a far more exceeding and eternal weight of glory" (2 Cor. 4:17).

- With Jesus you can bounce back.
- With Jesus you can make the rebound.
- With Jesus you can get up off the ground.
- With Jesus you can hold your heads up high.
- With Jesus you can be liberated, you can be delivered, you can be saved.
- No more defeat.
- No more guilt and shame.
- Victory, victory, victory!

Voices originally in the sermon dialogue were:
    Reverend Anthony Williams
    Deacon Michael Johnson
    Richard Clark
Voices of defeat and triumph were:
    1. Ralph Colbert, Sr.
    2. Marcus Jackson
    3. Elgie Henderson
    4. Barbara Jackson, Children's Work
    5. Alicia Butler
    6. Shirley McWilliams
    7. Queen Esther Shephard
    8. Herman Cox
    9. J. Alfred Smith, III

JAS, Jr.

16
How to Treasure the Treasure

John 1:12-13

Two days ago I thought I was back in my home state of Missouri. I arose early and turned on the water faucet, only to discover that there was no water. The first thing I did was wake up my wife and say, "Look, we don't have any water." And she said, "Well, I paid the water bill."

When I called the water company they explained that because of freezing weather my water pipes had frozen. My neighbors didn't know what to do, but because I didn't grow up in California, I knew how to thaw out the pipes. Before the day had expired my daughter had purchased some pipe insulation, but what you buy at the store doesn't always do the job. So, then I thought about how we used to survive before we realized that there was such a thing as pipe insulation. We took a rag and wrapped those pipes. Yesterday morning when I turned my water on, I saw that my neighbor's pipes had burst. That experience brought me closer to my text this morning. How strange it was that this experience with freezing water pipes, and not Christmas music, brought me closer to my text.

Not the Christmas songs, because Christmas songs romanticize the birth of Jesus. Christmas songs say that the night was a "Silent Night," it was a "Holy Night," but Christmas songs don't tell you how cold it really was. It was cold enough for someone to freeze, just like a homeless man froze to death last night in San Francisco. It was so cold that water in a little puddle would turn to ice. It was too cold for Heaven's Best, too cold for God's Treasure to be treated like trash, too cold for Jesus not to be born in a warm place. Jesus was born in a place where there was no thermostat, no central heating, no fireplace. He was born in a chilly place; where they didn't have running water; where they probably didn't have any water at all.

I'm talking about the birth of "God's Treasure." I'm talking about "God's Gift" to you and me. I'm talking about the birth of Jesus, our Savior. I'm speaking about the birth of One who can take all of us whose ideas are different and, at least, make us agree on the part that Jesus is the Savior of the world.

It's too bad that those mentioned in our text didn't know how to treat the Treasure. It's bad, because in Judea they had priests who had studied the sacred Scriptures. They knew that there was One who had been promised to cross fourteen generations and be the Savior of the world. But they must have been sleeping on their jobs. They should have been so steeped in prophecy that they could have told the people the Light was about to shine in darkness. They missed their opportunity. There was Herod with all of his royal power. He had his own army, his own cabinet, his own treasury department. He could have gone down in history if he would have rolled out the "red carpet" for God's treasure. But what did Herod do? He sent soldiers to kill all Jewish boys, two years old and under (see Matt. 2:16). Herod's government was guilty of genocide.

Sometimes I think that history has a way of repeating itself. Sometimes I see governments practicing genocide. I see governments going to war to make the profits of old men greater while the children of the poor die as soldiers. Sometimes they die because they are in the wrong country at the wrong time. Our Scripture reminds us that there are a few people who did not know how to treat the child like a treasure. They didn't even treat the child like trash because they didn't realize the worth of Jesus. They didn't know that the angel had spoken to Mary and said, "Mary, you are holding a little treasure in your arms, His name is Jesus, and He is going to save His people from their sins." They didn't know what was happening in history. There are people who awaken every day, travel to work, and return home after working, living repetitious and monotonous lives without ever recognizing what's happening in history.

But there were three men who knew what was occurring in history. The old preacher who didn't attend seminary would allegorize that fact and say of the three men, "One for the Father, and one for the Son, and one for the Holy Ghost." Wise Men from afar, from a strange place. How strange was that place? The magi probably came from the current home of Saddam Hussein, then Babylonia (now Iraq). These were no ordinary tourists, no mere travelers. These men were influential persons who could gain an audience with King Herod.

Ordinary persons just don't walk into a strange nation and announce, "I want to see the President." You must be influential in order to see the President. But these men, with King Herod's permission, came to see a baby. They didn't see Jesus as a baby— they saw him as a King. They traveled by faith. They had no knowledge of Mary and Joseph. They didn't know who they were, but they came by faith to see a baby who was not dressed like a king's baby. The Bible says He was "wrapped in swaddling clothes" (Luke 2:12). "Swaddling clothes" were not fancy.

But when the men from Saddam Hussein's country saw a baby dressed poorly they still fell down on their knees. They didn't judge the baby on the basis of His clothes, because they believed the ancient prophecy. Do we have that kind of faith? No doubt, some of us would have rejected God's treasure. First of all, He was born on the wrong street, in the wrong neighborhood. He was born on the wrong side of town, with the wrong color of skin, and dressed in the wrong kind of clothes, namely rags; in a place where there was no running water, lights, or furniture, there was God's Treasure.

Our skepticism would have asked, "What kind of foolishness is this? Maybe I misunderstood the revelation." No, you must believe God when you don't have evidence. You must trust God when you don't have all the facts. You must follow Him in the dark rather than to walk by yourself in the light. You must have faith like they did. They fell down on their knees and worshiped the child. Now, that's real faith. They were able to recognize that God works in mysterious ways. God doesn't transact Divine business like we do. And so they fell prostrate before Him and said, "We know how to treasure the Treasure." Each one had his gift. We ought to recognize what God gives us, and we ought to use what God gives us. I don't need to accentuate this stronger, but everyone of us has a gift unique unto ourselves. Therefore, my sisters and brothers, I may not be able to be an Anthony Williams (a member of Allen Temple), but if God had wanted more than one Anthony Williams, He would have made more than one. I may not have the musical touch of a Sam Matthews (also a member), but God wanted only one Sam Matthews. Each of us should accept the gifts the Lord has given us and use them for His honor.

I'm glad that they were men who were not jealous of one another. One man had gold; another, frankincense; and another, myrrh. But the man who had frankincense didn't become jealous of the man who had gold, he simply fell down at the baby's feet and gave the treasure he had. And that's all God expects of you. He doesn't expect you to compete with anybody else but yourself. Receive what God has given you and give it back to Him. Yes, I'm so glad that the man with frankincense didn't get upset because he didn't have gold. What do you use frankincense for? When a Jew gets ready to pray, he burns frankincense as incense which exemplifies prayer going up to God. Yes, Mary and Joseph needed gold. You need gold, and I need gold.

Our children need money for college tuition, shoes on their feet, clothes on their backs, medical insurance—but they also need some frankincense. Our children need prayer, I tell you. You can't be everywhere your child is. You need not only to have some money to educate that child, but you need your prayers and the prayers of others to help your child be what he ought to be. Then, last but not least, your child needs to learn how to pray for himself or herself.

Prayers have taught me that God can make a way out of no way. I know God can open doors that are shut in your face, make friends for you, fight your battles so you don't have to fight them at all. If you just call Him up and say, "Father, I stretch my hands to Thee; No other help I know; If Thou withdraw Thyself from me, Ah, whither shall I go?" So they gave that baby, gold, frankincense, and myrrh. Myrrh is for the sad times. Into every life some rain must fall. Every day is not going to be like Sunday. Sometimes you must climb the "Rough Side of the Mountain." Sometimes you have to bear your burden in the heat of the day. Sometimes you've got to climb Jacob's ladder. You can't ride the escalator. You've got to climb it, round by round. Sometimes you will have some sleepless nights, and you will need some myrrh to help you climb over. Yes, they gave the Treasure what the Treasure needed—gold, frankincense, and myrrh.

Herod was still after Jesus. The angel of the Lord told Joseph to take the baby and Mary and get out of Bethlehem. Go down to Egypt. "Out of Egypt have I called my son" (Matt. 2:15). Go down to Egypt. Well, "Lord, how am I going to get there?" Didn't the men from the East give some frankincense, some myrrh, and some gold? Take that gold, pay your way, and take care of Jesus until I tell you it's time to come home.

But if you will just treasure the Treasure, life for you will be whole. Whatever you do for Jesus will last. You know if you work in politics it will not last, but what you do for Jesus will last. You might go into business, the economy may get bad, and you may have to take out "Chapter 13," but what you do for the Lord will last. Jesus is God's Treasure. Treasure the Treasure. He will last.

If you will take your tangible treasures, they will have intangible continuity if you give them to the Master. If you take your tangible gifts and give them to the Lord, they will have intangible value. When the men fell down at Jesus' feet, and gave Jesus gold, frankincense, and myrrh, th·y had no way of knowing that all over the world, wherever the gospel is preached, the story would not be complete unless we tell what the wise men did for Jesus. Do it for Jesus and leave the result to God.

JAS, Sr.

17
The Joy of Giving

Acts 20:32-35

"It is more blessed to give than to receive" (v. 35). This simple verse, "It is more blessed to give than to receive," is a popular saying. It is one of the most well-known truisms in the Bible. In fact, it has become so well-known that it has slipped out of the pages of the Bible into the mainstream of idiomatic expressions. There are those who use the expression not knowing it is from the Bible.

I dare say there are even Christians who use the expression, knowing it came from the Bible, but not knowing who said it or where it can be found in this Book of divine truth. Therefore, let's take a moment to look at the context of this statement, the setting. "It is more blessed to give than to receive."

Just what was the situation that brought the apostle Paul to the point of using these words? If we look at the events leading up to this statement by Paul, we will notice that Paul had given up all that he had with the exception of his life, and he would soon give that up.

In the context of giving, Paul wrote to the Christians of Ephesus, "I commend you to God" (v. 32). Paul had worked until he had given all he had. The situation involved extreme danger for the apostle. Paul had been in a big skirmish, which almost broke out into a full-fledged riot because he dared speak of the glory and majesty of Jesus Christ. He came close to being killed. After having fled, going from Miletus to Ephesus, he preached with all that he had. He even preached all night long. We are told that he preached so long that one young lad, Eutychus, who was sitting on the windowsill, fell asleep and fell out of the window, dead, but God, through Paul, brought him to life.

When the young man was revived, Paul kept on preaching. He was on a mission. He gave 110 percent. Now he was making a farewell address to the elders of Ephesus. He was driven to go to Jerusalem to preach, even though the apostles had warned him that he would be jailed and eventually martyred if he made that trip. He was driven. He had to give everything he had in the service of our Lord. That was the situation in which Paul found himself—the events before and the events to follow—which makes the statement so significant.

It wasn't a routine kind of a situation. He wasn't just conversing with some people on a casual Saturday afternoon as the summer breeze blew through. Paul's life was hanging in the balances,and yet he could make this positive declaration to those whom God had entrusted to him. "I know that Jesus was right when He taught us, 'It is more blessed to give than to receive.'" Sometimes we face life situations, when we find ourselves questioning that truth. What benefit is there to give if all that is going to happen is I am going to be persecuted? Have you ever felt that?

How can I possibly preach that "It is more blessed to give than to receive" when everytime I try to give people stomp on it, throw it in the trash can, and slap me around? Have you felt that before? Why do I continue to give to my wife? Why do I continue to give to my husband? Why do I continue to give to these children? Why do I continue to try to do the right thing? Be a good community person? But we see from the example of the apostle Paul that regardless of the circumstances, we still somehow must be willing to give and give with joy.

Paul had given to "the last full measure of devotion." He was preparing to leave Ephesus and go give his body to the Lord. He testified to the elders, "I commend you to God." I don't have any silver and gold to give you. The best I can give to you, though—something that is more valuable—is a blessing, is a prayer. "I commend you to God." And I want to say to you sisters and brothers, that there are going to be situations where we have done all we can and we have nothing left to offer, and we are going to feel frustrated, and feel as if we are in a futile setting. We will feel like throwing our hands up, saying, "I wish I had something to give, but everything is gone from me." If you just offer up a prayer for that individual, if you just say, "I commend you to God," and you pray with fervor and sincerity, God will answer your prayer.

Don't leave anybody without a blessing. If nothing else, we can provide a blessing. As copastor, I run into situations that are bigger than I am. I see situations that members are in, and I feel so empathetic. But I'm only a small man. I can call on the phone. Deacons, you all know what I mean. You all do this, and you call this resource and call that resource—and you write letters and you go out and do whatever you can. Then you feel as if you are left with no resources, and all you have left to do is say, "Let's pray." We ought to pray in our families and commend one another to God. Commend our children to God. Don't give up on them. Don't throw them away. Commend them to God.

Then, as Paul continued his farewell address, he didn't just say "I commend you to God." That might have sounded cynical if left by itself. "I commend you to God." He made it clear that this was being offered in a positive manner. He stated, "God's grace will build you up and give you the blessing He has for His people." It says that right here in verse 32. That means, as you minister to that person, you can tell them, "No matter what you may have done—it may have been a sin that got you into your current predicament, and now you recognize the error of your way, and you want to make amends—don't worry about it. God's grace, that unmerited favor of God that looks beyond our thoughts and sees our needs, will intercede for you in your situation and provide you with the blessings He has for all of His people. If you run out of all your resources, give them a prayer, give them a blessing."

Paul moved on in verse 33 to share that he hadn't had a welfare mentality in doing ministry. He pointed out that he had not coveted anything they had. He wasn't doing ministry to gain silver, gold, clothing or any of that stuff. He was doing it because he was a servant of God. He was giving his life to God. Paul modeled for us the importance of having independence. He also modeled for us the importance of working, not feeling too good to work. And that's important for us who are in the church. We have to develop a self-sufficiency, and I don't want to use that term in the light to mean self-sufficiency from God. Yet, we need to recognize that God has gifted us with hands to work. He has gifted us with intelligence to work. He has gifted us with the ability to labor, do an honest day's work. And we have to live that out. But as we do, Paul made it clear that he was not putting down benevolences. He goes on to explain that by working hard he was not doing that merely to show he was so good and so mighty. He was doing that because he wanted to be able to help those who were weak and needy. Sisters and brothers, that's what we have to be about.

I can recall Pastor E. V. Hill of Mount Zion Baptist Church of Los Angeles sharing the illustration of God's blessings being like flowing waters. Dr. Hill declared that we cannot become so caught up in blessings God gives us that we build a dam where the blessings stop. He preached that we have to be a channel through which the blessings flow so others will be blessed by our blessings. If we are good stewards we recognize that what we receive via the blessings from God do not belong to us, but they are simply provided to us because God believes we will do His bidding to channel the blessings to others in need.

Yes, let's not be a dam which stops the blessings from flowing, but let us be a channel from which the blessings from God flow. Paul then asserts that there is more happiness in giving than receiving. I'm convinced that giving is natural, and giving is instinctive. Yet, we fight that natural instinct.

Have you ever watched a mother who nurses a baby? I think of the Cox family when they were here and the joy they had with that baby. Mothers so freely give to their babies, and there is joy in giving. I've actually seen mothers become upset when a doctor tells them they cannot nurse their baby.

Giving is natural and instinctive. Have you ever watched a small child, a little toddler, who may not even have learned to talk, and may be barely walking or crawling? Give that child a cookie, and that child will take that mushy, soggy cookie he or she had been sucking on, and try to give it to everybody in the room! It's natural. It's instinctive. God places something inside of us that makes us enjoy giving. There is a joy in giving. Let that child grow up, though, and become socialized, and the child forgets about giving. The child starts to develop selfish tendencies. We miss out on blessings because we are stingy. There's joy in giving. Giving has been a part of our African-American culture, but we are losing it. We come from a collectivist orientation where we don't have an individualistic identity, but we have a corporate identity, where we genuinely believe that if somebody else is hurt, we are hurting, too. If somebody else is joyous, we're joyous, too. Look at any of those traditional African societies, and you will see that collective spirit is built into the fabric of the culture. We have some of that left but we are in danger of losing it.

Some of the most generous people I know are senior citizens who grew up under that value system. They have less resources than anybody, but they give so freely. Those folk in the Bible class know what I am talking about, because there are some senior citizens in that class that are always giving. They take you under their wings, and they also have something nice to give. But many of us are losing our natural and cultural orientation which teaches us that giving is joy.

Giving must be joyous. It must come from a joyous attitude. It's not good enough just to give. The apostle Paul tells us that God loves a hilarious giver, a joyful giver. Have you ever been to lunch with those who fight you to pick up the tab? And some business psychologists claim that in some cases that isn't generosity, but a power play. Folks can become angry with you if you don't let them pick up the tab. We are not talking about that kind of an attitude and spirit.

Generosity in giving is not like a flu virus that infects church members. It is not contagious like a disease. It does not come as a plague that provides no escape from parishioners who appear in partnership for the preservation of pocketbooks. Paul goes on and says generosity is stewardship practiced at its best—not a prey to be chased or a contestant to be caught in the race of fund raising. Pastors cannot create giving churches by challenging unwilling members to give, cajoling, or by coaching consumer-oriented church members to place Christ before a culturally continued greed. Christ, the Master Teacher, made it plain in challenging pastors to teach Christians to observe the grace of giving—that grace of giving involves giving in an adopting attitude, giving not because it is going to evoke some sort of favor from somebody, but because it is just good to give. It feels good to give, and there is joy in giving. I can't preach one of those prosperity gospels that claims joy in giving emanates from being prosperous or even that giving leads to prosperity.

Joyous giving is the sharing of God-given joy. Because Christ has blessed you with spiritual and material gifts; because Christ has blessed you with love, joy, peace, forgiveness, faith, and hope; because Christ has given you life, health, and strength; because Christ has chosen you to serve on His program; because Christ has given you gifts to serve to the honor and glory of God; because God has smiled on you; because your cup of joy overflows in gratitude to God for blessings too numerous to count, you cannot help being a joyous giver.

The more you give of your time, talents, and treasure to the cause of Christ, the more you as a faithful steward will have to give joyously to Christ. How rich is the joy of giving? How inspirational is this joy of giving? To God be the glory, now and "world without end." Thanks be to God and to our Lord and Savior for the unspeakable and immeasurable joy of giving.

JAS, Jr.